Napoleon III and the Second Empire

IN THE SAME SERIES

General Editors: Eric J. Evans and P. D. King

LANCASTER PAMPHLETS

Napoleon III and the Second Empire

Roger Price

London and New York

First published 1997
by Routledge
11 New Fetter Lane, London EC4P 4EE

Simultaneously published in the USA and Canada
by Routledge
29 West 35th Street, New York, NY 10001

© *1997 Roger Price*

Typeset in Bembo by Routledge
Printed and bound in Great Britain by Clays Ltd, St. Ives PLC

British Library Cataloguing in Publication Data
A catalogue record for this book is available from the British Library

Library of Congress Cataloguing in Publication Data
A catalogue record for this book has been requested

ISBN 0–415–15433–2

In memory
of
Ralph Gibson
(1943–1995)

Contents

Preface

Ralph Gibson originally planned to write this book. Just before he died he was concerned that he would be unable to fulfil his commitment and gently reminded me that I had been preparing a book on the Second Empire for longer than either of us cared to remember. I hope that Ralph would have been happy with the result. It is written in memory of a very fine man, a considerable scholar and a very good friend.

Ralph arrived in this country from Adelaide as a young Rhodes Scholar in 1965. He returned to take up an appointment at the University of Lancaster in 1969 and remained there as Lecturer and, subsequently, Reader in History and French Studies until his untimely death in 1995. During this time he established an international reputation as a historian with such notable publications as *A Social History of French Catholicism, 1789–1914* (Routledge 1989); *Landownership and Power in Modern Europe* (in collaboration with Martin Blinkhorn, Harper-Collins 1991); 'The French nobility in the 19th century' in J. Howorth and P. Cerny (eds) *Elites in France* (Pinter 1981); 'Missions paroissiales et re-christianisation en Dordogne au 19e siècle' (*Annales du Midi* 1986); 'Hellfire and damnation in nineteenth-century France' (*Catholic History Review* 1988); 'De la prédication de la peur à la vision d'un Dieu d'amour' in *Le Jugement, le Ciel et l'Enfer dans l'histoire du christianisme* (Presses universitaires d'Angers 1989); 'Why Republicans and Catholics couldn't stand each other in nineteenth-century France' in F. Tallett and N. Atkin (eds) *Religion, Society and Politics: France, 1789–1945* (Hambledon Press 1991); 'Le Catholicisme et les femmes en France au

19e siècle' (*Revue d'Histoire de l'Eglise de France* 1993); 'The intensification of national consciousness in modern Europe' in C. Bjorn *et al.* (eds) *Nations, Nationalism and Patriotism in the European Past* (Copenhagen, Academic Press 1994); 'Théologie et société en France au 19e siècle' in J.-D. Durand (ed.) *Histoire et théologie* (Beauchesne 1994); and 'Female religious orders in nineteenth-century France' in F. Tallett and N. Atkin (eds) *Catholicism in Britain and France* (Hambledon Press 1996). The invitation to make a substantial contribution to G. Cholvy (ed.) *Matériaux pour l'histoire religieuse du peuple français, 19e–20e siècles*, Vol. III (Presses de la Fondation Nationale des Sciences Politiques 1992) offered clear recognition by French historians of his status both as a regional historian of the Dordogne and as an expert on religious history. If he had lived longer, Ralph would have amply confirmed his growing reputation with the two other major books he was working on: studies of *Women, Faith and Liberation: Female Religious Orders in nineteenth-century France* and of *Religion et Société: le diocèse de Périgueux au 19e siècle* (a massively expanded version of his French doctorate). Sadly, we shall be deprived of these, and of Ralph's witty and informed conversation and his unique sense of fun.

Acknowledgements

I would like to thank, in particular, Francesca Gibson for her kind assistance. Heather McCallum of Routledge and the series editors Eric Evans and David King were very encouraging and made helpful suggestions for revision of the first draft. The manuscript was carefully read and commented upon by: Colin Heywood of Nottingham University; Olena Heywood of the Open University; Aled Jones, my colleague in the Department of History and Welsh History at the University of Wales, Aberystwyth; and by Heather Price, whose constructive criticism, as always, was invaluable. Richard, Siân, Andy, Emily and Hannah provided help – and happy distractions.

Chronology

1848

23–24 February	Revolution and the establishment of the Second Republic; introduction of manhood suffrage
23 April	Election of a Constituent Assembly to prepare a new constitution
4 June	By-election victory by Louis-Napoléon Bonaparte
13 June	Debate in the Assembly on whether to admit the Bonapartist pretender to the throne as a deputy; admitted but resigns
23–26 June	Popular insurrection in Paris crushed
17 September	Louis-Napoléon re-elected
10 December	Election of Louis-Napoléon Bonaparte as President of the Republic

1851

2 December	Seizure of power by means of a military coup
21 December	Plebiscite ratifying extension of president's power

1852

14 January	Promulgation of new constitution
17 February	Press decree

29 February	Election of *Corps législatif*
25 March	Decree banning gatherings of more than 20 persons
27 March	End of martial law
21 November	Plebiscite on the re-establishment of the hereditary empire
2 December	Establishment of the Second Empire

1853

| 23 January | Haussmann appointed Prefect of the Seine |

1854

| 27 March | France and Britain declare war on Russia |

1856

| 16 March | Birth of the Prince-Imperial; remaining political prisoners amnestied on condition that they accept the regime |
| 30 March | Signature of Treaty of Paris ending the Crimean war |

1857

| 21 June | Election of new *Corps législatif* |

1858

14 January	Attempt to assassinate Napoléon by four Italians led by Orsini
27 February	Promulgation of general security law
14 June	End of state of emergency

1859

3 May	France declares war on Austria
11 June	Law regulating cooperation between state and railway companies
6 July	Franco-Austrian armistice leading to Treaty of Villafranca ends militarily successful campaign in Italy

1860

11 January	Publication of acrimonious correspondence between Emperor and Pope
22 January	Signature of Cobden–Chevalier commercial treaty with Britain
24 March	Treaty transferring sovereignty over Nice and Savoy to France
24 November	Publication of decree on political reform

1861

14 March	Emile Ollivier announces his willingness to rally to a liberal Empire
15 November	The Emperor promises financial reforms

1862

29 March	Franco-Prussian commercial treaty
16 April	Declaration of war on Juarez's government in Mexico

1863

23 May	Law authorising limited liability companies
31 May	General election
23 June	Designation of Minister of State as official government parliamentary spokesman

1864

11 January	Thiers in *Corps législatif* calls for 'the four necessary liberties'
25 May	Law establishing the right of workers to strike

1865

1 January	Government forbids the reading of parts of the Papal encyclical *Quanta Cura* and accompanying Syllabus of Errors from pulpits

1866

22 January	Announcement of decision to withdraw from Mexico
3 July	Decisive Prussian victory over Austria at Sadowa
12 December	Publication of controversial proposals for army reforms

1867

10–13 January	Talks between Napoléon and Ollivier
19 January	Publication of plans for further liberal reform
March	Presentation of proposed laws on the press and public meetings; promulgated 11 May and 6 June 1868, respectively

1868

March	French section of the Workers International prosecuted
31 March	Official tolerance of trade unions
May	Jules Ferry publishes *Les comptes fantastiques d'Haussmann*

1869

3 May	General elections begin
8–10 June	Serious disorders in Paris
16 June	Strike at Ricamarie, troops open fire
6 July	116 deputies support demands for a government responsible to parliament
12 July	Napoléon announces plans for further political reform
13 July	*Corps législatif* prorogued; resignation of Rouher
15 August	Unconditional amnesty for political offenders
27 December	Napoléon asks Ollivier to form a ministry

1870

2 January	Ollivier forms a government
5 January	Dismissal of Haussmann
26 February	Abandonment of official candidacy
21 March	Napoléon proposes to establish a liberal Empire
8 May	Plebiscite on proposals for constitutional reform
3 July	First news of Hohenzollern candidacy

19 July	France declares war on Prussia
26 July	Decision to withdraw protective French garrison from Rome; Italian troops enter the city on 2 September
10 August	Following initial military defeats, Cousin-Montauban (Comte Palikao) forms a conservative government
1–2 September	Defeat at Sedan and surrender of army led by the Emperor and MacMahon
4 September	Crowds enter the Palais Bourbon and republican deputies proclaim the Republic

Map   France in 1851

Source: *France 1848–1851*, Open University Press, 1976

1

Introduction

On 10 December 1848 the nephew of the great Emperor Napoléon was elected President of the French Republic, gaining a massive majority under the system of universal manhood suffrage introduced following the Revolution of the previous February. The origins of the Second Empire have to be searched for in the ruins of the first. The creation of a dynasty and foundation of a legend were two of the achievements of Napoléon I. Louis-Napoléon Bonaparte's major asset was undoubtedly his name, associating him with a Napoleonic cult kept alive throughout the intervening years by an outpouring of almanacs, pamphlets and lithographs promoting a legend of prosperity and glory. It had especial appeal in the countryside in which, it ought to be remembered, over 70 per cent of the population still lived. National pride had been incarnated in the historical memory of Napoléon. The July Monarchy (1830–48) had attempted to benefit by association. In 1833, the statue of the great Emperor had been replaced on top of the Vendôme column in the centre of Paris. In 1836, the Arc de Triomphe, celebrating the glorious achievements of the imperial armies, had finally been completed. The culminating event was undoubtedly the return, in 1840, of the remains of Napoléon I from Saint Helena to their final resting place in the Invalides. Vast crowds had turned out to watch the procession. Louis-Napoléon made every effort to take advantage of this powerful legend, deliberately conceived by the first Napoléon, diffused by the veterans of the Imperial armies, manufactured by printers, publishers and the producers of all manner of commemorative objects, and given respectability by the government of Louis-Philippe. At Strasbourg in 1836 and then Boulogne in 1840, Louis-Napoléon had attempted to seize power. He had appeared in uniform, behind a tricolour capped by an imperial eagle and sought to raise the local garrisons. Although pathetic failures in themselves, these adventures had at least helped to establish him in the public mind as the Bonapartist pretender. For much of the population, the Imperial years stood in marked contrast to the impoverishment and political strife which seemed to have accompanied its successor regimes. The misery of interminable war during the First Empire appeared largely to have been forgotten. Louis-Napoléon's electoral victory was evidence of the importance of historical myth but in the particular circumstances created by the long mid-century crisis, a complex series of inter-related economic and political crises with devastating social consequences. It was this situation which made it possible for Louis-Napoléon Bonaparte, previously known for his two adventurous but essentially mad-cap attempts to seize power through military coups, to finally succeed.

Varying approaches to the period

Historians have usually presented the Second Empire as a political drama in two acts. Their focus has primarily been on high politics and the character of Louis-Napoléon Bonaparte. The regime's ignoble origins in a *coup d'état* and the tragedy of its final humiliating collapse in the war of 1870 have loomed large. As ever, the approach taken by historians has been shaped by the concerns of their own time. At first, the dominant trend – as republicans struggled to secure the Third Republic (1870–1940) – was marked by bitter hostility. The combination of a carefully researched political narrative with moral indignation was exemplified by the journalist Eugène Ténot in two works on the *coup d'état*, published even before the Empire had disappeared. At its height in the 1930s and 1940s it identified Napoléon III as a precursor of Fascism. More positive assessments were also beginning to appear. Thus, from the inter-war years of the twentieth century and during the period of reconstruction following the devastation of World War II, historians' interests shifted to reflect a widespread concern about French 'backwardness' and 'stagnation'. They looked for lessons from what were judged to be the regime's constructive 'technocratic' achievements and, particularly, the reconstruction of Paris, the creation of a 'modern' transportation infrastructure and, more broadly, the establishment of the conditions for rapid economic growth. More recently, our knowledge of the period has been

2

enlarged considerably by social historians working at community or regional level. The traditional 'top down' approach to history with its focus on 'high' politics has been neatly supplemented by a 'bottom up' perspective much more concerned with the experience of the urban and rural masses.

State and society

The study of political leadership is undoubtedly of crucial importance; so too are questions about the nature of social and political systems. Their structures, both formal and informal, regulate the ways in which political authority can be exercised and provide environments for the creation of more diffuse political cultures. If the objectives political leaders set for themselves need to be identified, so too does the context within which they operate. The factors serving to reinforce or to restrict their authority are of obvious importance. It should be borne in mind also that governments are far from being unitary enterprises, but are frequently riven by internal rivalries and marked by a practical incapacity to achieve their objectives fully. Effectiveness depends in part on institutional design, but additionally on economic and social circumstances and frequently on the impact of largely uncontrollable external events. Thus, France during the Second Empire might be seen as a society in transition, undergoing (as so many parts of the contemporary developing world) an accelerating process of industrialisation and urbanisation, as part of which farming was increasingly commercialised and the rural world integrated into the national society. This might be described, without too much exaggeration, as the result of a communications' revolution, the product of the ongoing improvement of transport, of rising literacy levels and the development of the mass media. As a result, politics was not concerned simply with state–society relationships, but with the efforts of members of old and new elites to reach a compromise over the share of political power, as the vital means of securing their control over a rapidly changing, if still predominantly rural, world.

This pamphlet will attempt to build on the work of other historians and, most notably, that of Alain Corbin, Louis Girard, Vincent Wright and Theodore Zeldin (see Bibliography). While concentrating on a particular period and regime, the essential approach will remain problem orientated, although in the limited space available many crucially important questions will simply be noted rather than resolved. It will focus on the machinery of state, on the personnel involved (see also Price 1990: 27f), on policy formulation and upon its impact. Its initial emphasis, in

3

this introductory chapter, will be on state–society relations viewed from the perspective of the state. Its subject matter will include some of the central issues of socio-political history, including the identity of those individuals and social groups enjoying privileged access to the state apparatus. Obviously, 'the action of the state as an institution depends . . . on the people who direct it' (Birnbaum). These included the 'dictator' himself, Napoléon III, who enjoyed considerable personal power, as well as leading figures in the bureaucracy and military and influential members of the wider social elite from which they were recruited. Relationships between the Emperor and political elites as well as the internal dynamics of these groups will be one of our central concerns. The freedom of action of the head of state would vary considerably over time along with the willingness of these elites to accept his dominant position. Efforts to reinforce his authority and appeal over the heads of elites to the 'sovereign people' (employing such devices as the plebiscite together with electoral manipulation) enjoyed only limited success. As a result, some degree of agreement with (as well as substantial cohesion within) this political elite would appear to be a pre-requisite for effective state action. Other relevant questions include: What were the means by which its agents sought to legitimise their authority and how effective were they in penetrating society and in achieving their goals? How were the activities of state agencies perceived by the ruled and how did they respond as individuals and also as members of different social and regional groups? This process of interaction, both with the state and each other, occurred within a society which remained profoundly inegalitarian. Inevitably, the capacity for political mobilisation varied considerably. Moreover, overt and straightforward class conflict was only episodic and offers only a very imperfect guide to analysis. As a result, a wide range of additional questions suggest themselves. The list that follows is far from inclusive. It needs, however, to include at least the following: What were the effects of government policy and a concurrently accelerating process of industrialisation on a social system combining 'archaisme et modernité' (Corbin 1975)? How did the perceived need to promote economic development affect the regime's agenda? To what extent did economic 'modernisation' and most obviously the revolution in communications affect the government machine and particularly its capacity to penetrate society? Conversely, how did social change and a widespread (although very unequal improvement) in living standards influence political attitudes? What was the impact of the establishment of an authoritarian and repressive political regime followed, after a decade, by liberalisation, the easing of restrictions on political activity, and (re-)politicisation? To what extent did politics involve competition between elite groups for access to political power and patronage and to what extent did it represent a challenge, from below, to the established social order? Lastly, how did internal and external politics interact?

Similar questions might be asked of any political system. Every regime is responsible, primarily, for the maintenance of order, although definitions of what constitutes 'order' and the systems constructed and methods employed to achieve this objective will vary both between regimes and, in the case of the same regime, over time as situations and personnel change. Political repression can be regarded as a 'normal' feature of governmental activity, but its intensity varies with perceptions of danger and the capacity of the administration to conduct 'police' measures. Thus, the establishment of the Second Empire or, for that matter, Fascist Italy or Nazi Germany might in part be seen as responses to particularly intense general crises and widespread social fear. Repression, however, carries the risk of alienating much of the subject population. The Second Empire can be distinguished from the two twentieth-century dictatorships because, by means of liberalisation and the institutionalisation of protest through elections, it sought a method of moderating opposition and of more effectively ensuring long-term stability. In this context, the criteria employed for defining potential threats and ensuing policy decisions – as between repression or concession – tell us a great deal about a regime and its relationships with the wider society. It is probably true that most regimes would prefer to rule through forms of social control which encourage consensus and possess a clearly defined moral and legal basis for the exercise of power, rather than resort to violence. This explains the importance of securing cultural domination through religious or educational institutions which provide means of instruction designed to induce conformity to socially and politically conservative norms of behaviour.

The debate on the nature of the state and, indeed, on the character of the Second Empire continues to be informed by the contribution of Karl Marx. In *The Manifesto of the Communist Party* (1848), he contended that 'the executive of the modern state is but a committee for managing the common affairs of the whole bourgeoisie'. The forms taken by a state were the product of class rule at a particular stage of social development. His stress on the repressive role of the state was supplemented by an insistence on the state's employment of religion and patriotism and on its recourse to war, as a means of reinforcing its position – an emphasis foreshadowing the Italian Marxist Gramsci's

5

notion of hegemony. However, Louis-Napoléon Bonaparte's seizure of power caused problems for Marx. It represented an apparent renunciation of power by the 'ruling classes' and a step back from bourgeois liberalism to absolute monarchy, to a situation in which 'the executive power with a host of officials numbering half a million, besides an army of another half a million, [an] appalling parasitic body . . . enmeshes the body of French society like a net and chokes all its pores' (Marx 1848: 284–5). The state had achieved apparent autonomy. This seeming contradiction could be resolved only by insisting that the state continued to favour the interests of some social groups rather than others. It remained the guarantor of the established social order. Marx assumed that, in the longer term, state policy had to remain compatible with the interests of economically and socially powerful interest groups, particularly those from which ministers, bureaucrats and army officers were recruited (Marx 1962: 340–1). Awareness of context is all important. The rulers of a nineteenth-century authoritarian state could deal harshly with opponents, but were neither willing nor able to engage in the forms of extreme and sustained brutality which have been employed to ensure compliance during the twentieth century. While the elites which had shared political power during the Restoration (1814–30) and July Monarchy (1830–48) might be prepared to accept a temporary dictatorship at a time of extreme crisis (in the fashion of the ancient Roman Republic with which these classically educated elites were so familiar), in the longer term they would favour a return to a 'normal' and renewed fragmentation of political power. In effect, the boundaries to state action were defined partly by power centres – social groups, political alliances, institutional bodies – capable of political organisation. Stability depended upon accommodating their special interests. As a result of the introduction of manhood suffrage following the revolution in February 1848, greater attention would also be given to the concerns of socially subordinate groups: to the small businessmen, professionals, peasants and workers all increasingly anxious to influence state policy. Indeed, one of the central questions to be considered in this essay will be the degree to which these various groups might have lost or benefited from changes in the (unequal) balance of power. Another concern will be the ways in which state power impinged upon the various groups and how they perceived its activities – as class oppression or as the benign exercise of authority. How would they react, not only to governmental activity, but also to social change on a previously unimagined scale? While continuities with the past will frequently need to be stressed, contemporaries could hardly fail to be aware of the tearing down and reconstruction of city centres, of railway lines and telegraph wires extending their tentacles across the landscape and creating new opportunities for enrichment, but within a far more competitive environment. More than ever before, people were on the move in search of a better life. What were the relationships between economic and social change, the 'formal' establishment of manhood suffrage, and the evolution of local and national political cultures? Certainly, historically-based expectations conditioned individual political behaviour to a large degree. The Second Empire is of particular interest, however, because in a relatively short time radical changes in economic structures and political institutions forced people to adapt their life strategies.

Sources

The sources for this study are many and varied, and all of them have their shortcomings. In preparation for a much more substantial volume on the Second Empire currently being written, an effort has been made to consult as wide a range of sources as possible, including private papers, memoirs, administrative reports, official and private economic and social enquiries, and the newspaper press. As always, the directly expressed views of the masses are greatly under-represented. Much of the surviving information on them is derived from the observations of members of other social groups and is inevitably distorted by their particular concerns and prejudices. Reporters from the social elites tended to focus in particular on novelty and whatever appeared to be threatening to their interests. Government officials frequently told their superiors what it was presumed they wanted to hear in the hope of enhancing their career prospects. Newspaper reports were rarely unbiased. The quality of reporting obviously varied according to individual skills and commitment. A massive amount of information was gathered by more or less zealous and competent officials operating within the various established administrative hierarchies (especially those reporting to the Ministers of the Interior, Justice and War) to be interpreted, passed upwards and incorporated in ever more general situation reports. Complaints about the quality of reports were frequent, especially about the unwillingness of those at the bottom of the hierarchy – mayors, justices of the peace and gendarmes – to spare the time and effort. Experience suggests that the recruitment, training and professional concerns of the judicial administration (particularly the state prosecutors – the *procureurs généraux*) resulted in more objective and frequently more

7

comprehensive reports than those emanating from the parallel prefec-toral hierarchy. Election results distorted by governmental and also elite social pressures are similarly difficult to interpret, particularly in the absence of formal organised parties. 'Parties' were little more than informal associations of individuals with shared aspirations and ideas. Voting decisions were informed by the competing influence of govern-ment officials, local notables and the clergy, as well as by shifting mass perceptions of what was at issue and the relevance of particular policies to their own needs. The candidates for election were invariably chosen either by ministers and prefects or by self-selected committees adhering to one or another political persuasion. They were selected from among those mature adult males judged to possess the personal, educational and rhetorical qualities believed necessary for serious participants in public life. By definition, the mass of the population – women as well as the poorly educated lower middle classes, workers and peasants – was judged to be unsuitable and this, in general, by their own kind as well as the upper classes.

Phases of development

Events were profoundly marked by the personality of the Emperor. An initial assessment of the character and abilities of this nephew of the great Napoléon is clearly necessary. In his 1869 preface to *The Eighteenth Brumaire of Louis Bonaparte*, Marx observed that his purpose was to 'demonstrate how the class struggle in France created circumstances and relationships that made it possible for a grotesque mediocrity to play a hero's part' (Marx 1962: 244). The accession to power of an individual widely regarded by his contemporaries as lacking ability and principles inevitably caused surprise and disquiet. Alexis de Tocqueville, who would serve briefly as foreign minister following Bonaparte's election to the presidency, recognised his courage and determination, but was hardly less scathing, pointing out that 'a dwarf on the summit of a great wave is able to scale a high cliff which a giant placed on dry ground at the base would not be able to climb' (Price 1972: 323–4). It was the intense mid-century crisis which had created an opportunity for the Bonapartist pretender.

These were negative judgements of an adventurer who, in terms of background, education and experience, did not fit into conventional moulds. Another well-connected politician, Charles de Rémusat, pointed out that 'He lacks all the qualities of an ordinary man of merit, judge-ment, instruction, conversation, experience, all of these things are so lacking that one is tempted to assume that he is beneath contempt. But this idiot is endowed with a rare and powerful faculty – that of placing himself at the centre of human affairs . . . His presence has changed the course of history . . . Whoever is able to intervene in the affairs of the world and impose and produce or modify events according to his will possesses I don't know what gift of daring or strength which sets him apart from the crowd and places him amongst the rank of historical personalities' (Rémusat 1962: 359–60). Personality is at least as much the product of private as of public experience. As a result of his family background and upbringing, Louis-Napoléon Bonaparte possessed an intense sense of personal destiny and faith in his historical mission. In his determination to become guardian of the Napoleonic tradition, he combined the outlook of a romantic mystic with the instincts of a political opportunist. Understanding him is not easy and requires the close analysis of his writings and speeches as well as of the views of those few relations and collaborators who managed to get close to this very private person. His friend from childhood, Mme. Cornu, in conversation with the well-connected British political economist Nassau William Senior, described his 'mission' as 'a devotion first to the Napoleonic dynasty, and then to France . . . His duty to his dynasty is to perpetuate it. His duty to France is to give her influence abroad and prosperity at home' (Senior 1878 II: 115). Even when he relaxed with such old friends, his manner made it impossible for them to forget his rank. Moreover, he rarely spoke openly and unambiguously, and outside this narrow circle most contemporary assessments were provided by political critics.

Louis-Napoléon's objectives would be spelled out in a letter to his cousin Napoléon-Jérôme: 'When one bears our name and is head of government, there are two things to do: satisfy the interests of the masses, and secure the loyalty of the upper classes.' This would require a constant juggling act. His basic ideas were stated quite early in his career in a series of pamphlets. These included most notably *Les Reflections politiques* (1832), *Les Idées napoléoniennes* (1839) – based closely on the writings of Napoléon I and on Las Cases' *Mémorial* – and *L'Extinction du paupérisme* (1844). Although the presentation was vague, imprecise and replete with contradictions, these writings, reflecting the utopian optimism of the 1830s and 1840s, were to serve as his 'guiding ideas' (Plessis 1985: 9–10, quoting a letter from Napoléon to Walewski in early 1859). His objectives can be characterised by a determination to eliminate the party divisions created by the French Revolution which he believed were responsible for political instability. As heir to the glories of the First Empire, he saw himself as the incarnation of patriotic unity. The role of a

9

future emperor, his authority legitimised by 'universal suffrage', would be to represent the nation. Although sharing with conservatives a determination to safeguard public order, Louis-Napoléon was distinguished by this apparent commitment to 'popular sovereignty'. Periodic plebiscites would serve to ratify the regime's general policies, as well as to re-affirm the 'mystical link between Emperor and people' (Campbell 1978: 4). Through its vote the people would delegate power to the Emperor and legitimise his authority (Emerit 1937: 198). The powers of representative assemblies – representative only of the particular interests of deputies (letter to Cornu, quoted in Girard 1986: 30) – were to be reduced to a minimum. A commitment to the principles of 1789, and particularly to equality before the law and to popular sovereignty, was thus combined with belief in the need for strong, centralised government. He assumed confidently that only the Bonapartist dynasty could represent effectively these twin principles of order and democracy. Internal and external policies would be closely related. Revenge for the defeats of France by the allies in 1814–15 and a rejection of the stipulations of the Peace of Vienna which followed were the essential means of reinforcing both the legitimacy of a future restored empire and the glory of France.

Our immediate need will be to consider the significance of the mid-century crisis (1846–51) which created the circumstances in which Louis-Napoléon Bonaparte was able, first to secure election to the powerful position of President of the Republic and, subsequently, to make use of the authority of this office in order to seize more permanent and unrestricted power through the re-establishment of the hereditary empire first created by his illustrious uncle. This Second Empire has usually been divided into two phases by historians – *the authoritarian* in which decisions were largely taken by the Emperor and his close advisors, ministers were responsible to the monarch rather than to a parliament which had very limited powers, the press strictly censored, political meetings banned, election results manipulated, and protest firmly repressed by police action, and *the liberal* resulting from a gradual easing of the restrictions on political activity. However, in spite of the onset of reforms from 1860, the regime remained far from liberal until the introduction of far-reaching constitutional reform in 1869. The repeated descriptions of growing political difficulties, rising opposition, together with the exhaustion and increasing irresolution of the Emperor and leading ministers seems to offer a clear linear vision of inevitable collapse. However, this approach ignores the very real problems of regime transition once the regime's leading figure(s) had taken the decision(s) to adapt to changing political circumstances. Would reforms which freed political activity and allowed strikes, and which thereby created a sense of expectancy and demands for further change, provoke the collapse or, by reducing discontent, promote the re-consolidation of the regime? The current problems of post-Communist Russia illustrate the difficulties of transition from authoritarian to more democratic political systems.

2

Louis-Napoléon Bonaparte, President of the Second Republic

The February Revolution of 1848 and its aftermath

The Revolution which overthrew the regime of Louis-Philippe (the so-called July Monarchy) and led to the establishment of a Second Republic (1848–52) brought to power through acclamation by the crowds of insurgents a Provisional Government composed of ministers, headed by the aristocratic poet Alphonse de Lamartine, who owed their republican credentials to parliamentary and journalistic activity. Inexperienced and cautious and being largely men of some substance themselves, they were determined to restore order to the streets and to resist pressure for immediate and substantial social reform. Instead of taking the political initiative, they preferred to await the election of a Constituent Assembly which would prepare a new republican constitution. This would be elected by manhood suffrage, a concession ministers had felt bound to make and which inaugurated a new era in politics, replacing as it did the very restricted electorate of previous regimes. The results were far from those which radical republicans and socialists had dreamed about and conservatives dreaded. The April elections saw the nomination by the predominantly small town and rural electorate of a parliament with a large majority of moderate republican and conservative deputies drawn from the educated, property-owning classes. They, too, were anxious to re-establish public order which had been disturbed by the revolution and the immense wave of expectancy it had created among the impoverished popular classes, particularly the relatively politicised Parisian lower-middle and working classes. Radical republicans, anxious to promote further democratisation and far-reaching social reform, were dismayed. A clash was unavoidable. The decision in June to close the Parisian National Workshops provided the occasion. These had been established by the Provisional Government as a means of providing work relief for the mass of unemployed. Recovery from the extremely severe crisis caused by successive poor cereal harvests and potato disease from 1845, and intensified by declining demand for manufactured goods and lack of confidence among investors, had been well underway by February 1848. However, the economic situation had deteriorated sharply again as a result of the crisis of confidence caused by the revolution itself. The Workshops, which had been for the new moderate republican ministers a temporary expedient, were viewed by socialist intellectuals and many workers as the first step in a thorough re-casting of society, resulting from the creation of a network of producer cooperatives. Their dream was to eliminate the capitalist employer and the exploitation of labour. The government's decision to close the National Workshops in order to secure financial savings and balance the budget as well as to eliminate large and increasingly threatening daily gatherings of workers thus had enormous symbolic as well as practical significance. The final effort in Paris to resist the 'reactionary' tendencies of the government took the form of the June insurrection in which political radicals and workers, drawn mainly from the ranks of the skilled artisanal crafts, sought to seize power. Their rising was crushed brutally by military forces mobilised by the moderate republican government and commanded by its defence minister, General Cavaignac. Even then, the threat to social order which had so frightened the propertied classes did not disappear entirely. Democrats and socialists continued to organise. Economic conditions remained depressed. There was widespread fear of another attempted insurrection. Conservative publicists combined historical experience with myth to create a nightmare vision of social revolution involving not only a repetition of the Terror of 1793, but also the total dispossession of the propertied classes. This unmistakably informed their political behaviour. In this situation, it appeared essential to most of the deputies engaged in preparing the new constitution that the country be provided with a president possessing wide powers and the authority derived from popular sovereignty. The result would be the election on 10 December 1848 of the nephew of the great Emperor as President of the Republic.

The Presidential elections

When he first stood as a candidate in by-elections in June and September 1848, Louis-Napoléon had enjoyed substantial success in spite of little press support or organisation. Conservative leaders and journalists had ridiculed him initially, but this contempt for the Bonapartist pretender turned into an opportunistic and qualified adherence as it became evident that he was likely to attract substantial popular electoral support often, and alarmingly, in spite of the advice to voters from their social 'superiors'. The British ambassador Lord Normanby wrote that 'history affords no parallel to this spectacle of all the eminent men of all former political parties uniting in support of a man whom not one of them would personally have selected. They, in fact, follow whilst they assume to direct, a popular impulse which they could not resist' (Normanby 1851 II: 361). Social elites were largely divided between squabbling monarchist factions – the Legitimist supporters of the Bourbons driven into exile following the July Revolution of 1830 with their ideological commitment to absolutist, hierarchical, paternalistic and theocratic political and social systems, and the Orleanist supporters of Louis-Philippe, deposed in February 1848, equally conservative in terms of their attitudes towards social reform, but liberal in their greater individualism and confidence in the virtues of parliamentary representation based on a restricted suffrage. The leaders of these factions were unable to reach agreement on a candidate likely to defeat Louis-Napoléon and came increasingly to support his candidature. This tactic would at least reduce the impact of their divisions and allow them to take advantage of his popularity. It would additionally facilitate the struggle against what they believed was a growing socialist menace. Most conservative politicians saw the Bonapartist prince as a weakling, a clown they could use. Thiers quipped contemptuously 'We will give him women and we will lead him' (quoted by Dansette 1961: 243). In the absence of a significant group of Bonapartist notables, it seemed certain that if elected he would continue to depend upon their support. Moreover, he appeared to be committed to the restoration of social order. At the very least his election would prevent the consolidation of the republic. Influential figures among the former leaders of the 'loyal' or 'dynastic' opposition to Louis-Philippe such as Molé, Barrot and, most notably, Thiers played an especially important role in rallying conservatives. The only real alternative, the moderate republican General Cavaignac, possessed the merit of having suppressed the June insurrection, but he was still too much of a republican for most conservatives. He attracted support from the port

Table 2.1 Results of Presidential elections, 10 December 1848

Louis-Napoléon Bonaparte	5, 534, 520 (74.2%)
General Cavaignac	1, 448, 302
Ledru-Rollin (radical republican)	371, 431
Raspail (socialist)	36, 964
Lamartine (moderate republican)	17, 914
General Changarnier	4, 687

cities in which the 'black' legend of the economic disaster caused by the British maritime blockade during the Empire was still strong, and from some Legitimist and clerical regions, e.g. Morbihan and Finistère in Brittany and Bouches-du-Rhône in the south-east which remained bitterly hostile to Bonapartism. As if to illustrate the complexity of voting behaviour, these same groups in departments like Tarn and Tarn-et-Garonne voted for Bonaparte against Cavaignac, who was condemned by both his republicanism and the support of local Protestant elites. Many of the more radical republicans also felt unable to support the major republican candidate. In their eyes he would remain the 'butcher of June'. Frequently, they appear to have believed that Napoléon I had continued the work of the revolution and failed to see a vote for his self-proclaimed heir as entirely incompatible with their own republican principles. This was the great strength of the Bonapartist legend. It allowed Louis-Napoléon to present himself as 'all things to all men', as a leader above existing party struggles. His victory in December was overwhelming (see Table 2.1).

In Paris Louis-Napoléon gained 58 per cent of the votes cast but, significantly, support for the author of the apparently socialistic pamphlet on the *Extinction du paupérisme* was highest in the popular *quartiers* in which both before and even during the June insurrection there had already been plenty of evidence of Bonapartist sentiment. The democrat and former Interior Minister Ledru-Rollin and the socialist Raspail shared a mere 12.4 per cent of the vote, a pattern repeated in most large cities. However, in spite of this strong showing, it was the rural vote which would continue to provide the bedrock of Bonaparte's popular support for the next two decades.

Louis-Napoléon Bonaparte, Prince-President

Following his appointment, the new president named a government made up mostly of former Orleanists headed by Odillon Barrot. This appeared to confirm to the supporters of the conservative alliance, the so-called 'Party of Order', that they could rely on his subservience. However, more perceptive observers like the Austrian diplomat Apponyi were already observing that 'if they believe themselves able to do anything with him and to dominate him, they are badly mistaken' (Apponyi 1948: 78). The essential objective of these monarchist ministers remained the restoration of order. In the short term, repression depended upon police action against left-wing political activists. Following the June insurrection, a series of laws and bureaucratic processes which restricted political activity were introduced. They provided the legal basis for both an increasingly authoritarian republic and the Imperial regime which would follow it. For the longer term, conservatives looked forward to the moral re-education of the population. The objective of a new education law introduced in March 1850 (the *loi Falloux*) was defined by Michel, a member of the extra-parliamentary committee which prepared it, as being 'to train a child to the yoke of obedience, to create in him a principle of energy which will enable him to resist his passions, accept of his own free will the law of labour and duty and contract habits of order and regularity . . .' (Price 1972: 254). Deferential behaviour was to be internalised by the young. The essential agents of this were to be the clergy. The notorious anti-clerical Adolphe Thiers, another member of the preparatory committee, insisted on this with breathtaking cynicism. Priests would be encouraged both to teach and to supervise a thoroughly purged secular teaching force, the members of which would also be expected to inculcate a conservative and intensely religious ideology. The clergy responded very positively to this opportunity to increase their influence, but at the cost of a considerable intensification of anti-clericalism on the left. More immediately, an effort was made to restore social order through the continuous tightening of repressive measures directed at a left united, from the Autumn of 1848, under the *démocrate-socialiste* banner. This led to the demobilisation of many of its intimidated supporters, to the fragmentation of its organisation as the more persistent activists were driven underground, and to the bankruptcy of most of its newspapers as a result of repeated fines and suspensions. The election of a substantial minority of *démocrate-socialiste* deputies in the May 1849 general elections, as well as in subsequent by-elections, nevertheless revealed that the threat from the left was far from dead. In particular, its ability to attract support in some rural areas, especially in the south-east, reinforced old concerns about the principle of manhood suffrage. The apparent unreliability of peasant support for the conservative cause created the nightmare possibility of victory by the left in both the legislative and presidential elections due in 1852. It was intolerable, according to the state prosecutor at Rouen, that 'the communists [be offered] the possibility of becoming kings one day by an electoral *coup d'état*. Society must not commit suicide'. The provincial newspaper *L'Opinion* of Auch echoed many others in asking whether 'the fate of a great nation [can] be abandoned to this blind power . . . ?' It concluded that 'Universal suffrage will bring the ruin of France'. Legislation was introduced on 31 May 1850 which imposed new preconditions for electoral registration, including three years' prior residence in a constituency, the absence of a criminal record, and 'eligibility' to pay the personal tax. This disqualified 31.4 per cent of the electorate at a stroke and, as was intended, much higher proportions in the industrial and major urban centres. Significantly, if he did not oppose the new law, the President distanced himself publicly from this legislation, leaving all the running in its preparation to the monarchist majority in parliament. Although this legislation seemed likely to guarantee their electoral success in 1852, it did little to reduce conservative hysteria. *Démoc-soc* propaganda encouraged the disenfranchised to seize their rights, weapons in hand if necessary, on election day. Although repression enjoyed considerable success and fear of persecution forced many republicans out of politics, *démoc-soc* organisation survived in fragmented form. This was particularly true in under-policed rural regions of the centre and south in which substantial mass support had previously been built up. There, domiciliary searches, arbitrary arrests and continued interference by the administration in communal affairs bred resentment. Repression drove remaining *démoc-soc* militants underground, forcing them to use traditional forms of popular sociability such as cafés and private drinking clubs as cover. This radicalisation of the *démoc-soc* movement further heightened official anxiety about plots by secret societies to seize power by force.

The impact of repression was also weakened by the tension which continued to exist between the various monarchist factions, in spite of their shared fear of social revolution. Memories of past conflicts, ideological divisions, personal rivalries and suspicion of the Prince-President's ambitions ensured that the Party of Order remained divided. Bonapartism, although enjoying considerable popular support, gained little sympathy among the political elites. Yet, as the prospect of a *démoc-soc* electoral victory in 1852 drew closer, as the 'red spectre' became ever more real and rumours of socialist plots were given greater credence, the willingness of notables to accept more extreme measures to preserve 'order' became increasingly pronounced. In this anxious and economically depressed climate more and more people looked to the President of the Republic for a solution. As head of state, Louis-Napoléon controlled the government machine and the army which was, before the creation of a modern police, the essential means of securing internal order. His position was reinforced by the inability of Legitimists and Orleanists, as in 1848, to agree on an alternative candidate for the 1852 presidential elections. Bonaparte's problem was that provisions of the constitution barred him from standing for a second successive term in office and there were a sufficient number of republicans in the Assembly to prevent constitutional revision by the necessary two-thirds majority. His utter determination to retain power left him with little choice but to attempt a third *coup d'état* and, on this occasion, from a position of strength.

The Presidential coup d'état

The coup, which took place on 2 December 1851, was directed against both the republicans and the monarchist groups represented in parliament. The fact that only the former offered armed resistance, and that conservatives tended to welcome the President's seizure of power, gave it an overwhelmingly anti-republican character. Thus, it might be seen as the culmination of a long period of political repression, with the extension of martial law to the entire country facilitating the final destruction of the *démoc-soc* movement. Mounting the coup proved to be relatively easy for the head of government of a centralised state in which army officers and officials were committed to passive obedience. It had been carefully planned by the President and his closest advisors. Trusted personnel had been moved into key positions, notably the President's half-brother, the Comte de Morny, to the Interior Ministry and General Saint-Arnaud to the War Ministry. In implementing the coup, the semaphore telegraph system, reserved for official use, allowed the government a considerable time advantage for the despatch of instructions and receipt of information. Preventative arrests of monarchist leaders like Adolphe Thiers, the Generals Changarnier, Bedeau and Lamoricière, and republicans who might be tempted to organise resistance, had been carefully planned. On 30 November a practice alert had even allowed a military rehearsal. The tactic was to concentrate troops in the major urban centres and garrison towns and, once their security had been assured, to deploy mobile columns into the countryside. The practical disadvantage of this plan was that it would allow time for insurrections to develop in some disaffected and under-policed small towns as well as in surrounding rural areas.

In Paris there was only very limited resistance to the coup. This was because of obvious military preparations and partly due to preventative arrests. Conservative deputies vied with each other for the privilege of being arrested and absolved of any further responsibility in the affair. There were appeals to rally to the defence of republican institutions launched by a small group of republican deputies including such luminaries as Victor Hugo, Hippolyte Carnot, Jules Favre, Michel de Bourges and Victor Schoelcher, and additionally by Jules Leroux and August Desmoulins on behalf of workers associated with a *comité central des corporations*. None the less, few workers were prepared to risk a repetition of the slaughter which had followed the June insurrection, particularly in defence of the sovereignty of a parliament dominated by monarchists who had deprived many of them of the right to vote. Moreover, the President still enjoyed the personal prestige of his Bonapartist inheritance and, in the proclamation which justified the coup, promised the immediate restoration of manhood suffrage. Nevertheless, on 3 and 4 December, demonstrations (mainly involving workers) occurred and some 70 barricades were constructed in the rue du Faubourg-Saint-Antoine and in the old centres of popular revolution in the streets adjoining the rues Saint-Denis, Rambuteau and Transnonain. The army did not repeat the mistakes of February 1848 and again, as in June, deployed large, concentrated formations, well supplied with provisions and ammunition. Around 30, 000 troops faced some 1, 200 insurgents. This unequal struggle was inevitably short lived. Subsequently, the official newspaper, the *Moniteur universel* announced that 27 soldiers and 380 civilians had been killed, although the second figure was inflated by the casualties caused when panicking soldiers fired volleys at peaceful, and mainly middle-class, spectators along the boulevards Bonne-Nouvelle, Poissonnière, Montmartre and des Italiens.

Short-lived demonstrations also occurred in many other towns. In Lille, the republican newspaper *Messager du Nord* on 3 December launched a call for resistance and, in the evening, workers gathered on the *grande-place*. They were easily dispersed. News of the failure of resistance in Paris discouraged further action. To take another example, in eastern France, Dijon, a crowd of 400–500 people gathered outside the railway station in the afternoon of 3 December to wait for news from Paris. The local *démoc-soc* leadership was, however, mostly arrested while waiting at a printer's for leaflets calling for resistance to be printed. Militants in Dijon itself and in Beaune and other small towns in the region who habitually followed their lead remained inactive. Their hesitancy was in marked contrast with the obvious determination of the authorities. From the government's point of view, the situation was, unexpectedly, to become far more serious in the provinces than in the large towns. Some 100, 000 men from around 900 communes were involved in various forms of protest; as many as 70, 000 from at least 775 communes actually took up arms and over 27, 000 participated in acts of violence (Margadant 1979). Insurrections occurred where *démoc-soc* militants had succeeded in appealing to popular conceptions of justice, linking their political programme to widespread practical grievances and, above all, where organisational structures centred on small towns and market villages had survived repression. Risings occurred in the centre (Allier, Nièvre); south-west (Lot-et-Garonne, Gers) and especially the south-east (Drôme, Ardèche, Basses-Alpes, Hérault, Var) – i.e. in a minority of rural areas south of a line Biarritz–Pithiviers (Loiret)–Strasbourg. These were regions in which small-scale peasant farming predominated and which were experiencing the effects of growing population pressure on the land. The difficult situation within them was made all the worse by the persistent difficulties of market-orientated activities like vine and silk cultivation, forestry and rural manufacture. To the north and west of this line, in the departments of western France, the north, north-east and most of the Paris region, there was little disorder. These were mostly either areas of larger-scale commercial farming in which more advanced industrial development did something to relieve population pressure, or zones in the west characterised by economic backwardness and intense poverty. They were regions in which traditional elites, generally enjoying the support of the church, retained considerable influence.

The insurrections provided further justification for a settling of accounts. Over 26, 000 *démoc-soc* militants were arrested throughout France, rather than simply where insurrections had occurred. The authorities were anxious to eliminate the radical republican leadership, irrespective of whether individuals had been involved in resistance to the coup or not. The official statistics on those arrested revealed that 10.6 per cent belonged to the middle-class professions (including 1, 570 rentiers, 325 doctors and 225 lawyers) and that the largest group were artisans and workers in the traditional trades (builders, shoemakers, tailors, etc.), followed by peasants (5, 423 *cultivateurs*, 1, 850 *journaliers*, etc.), although peasants made up a far higher proportion of the rank-and-file (Price 1972: 289). The coup allowed the authorities to complete the work of repression without paying too much attention to the rule of law. The fright they had received, their bitter hatred of the left and their inability to comprehend its motives is evident from the insulting phraseology contained in the interrogation records. The insurrection was explained by the authorities in terms of the poor and ignorant being led astray by the greedy, envious and perverted. That many of the *démoc-soc* leaders were educated and comparatively well-off bourgeois, were in effect class traitors, was almost beyond comprehension. Throughout France republican leaders were arrested, exiled or discredited. Their followers, if they had been arrested, were usually soon released, but most had been frightened into political quiescence, throwing themselves on the mercy of the authorities as the only means of protecting themselves from retribution, and the terrifying arbitrariness of police and military action. The contrast between this situation and their dreams of the social and democratic republic which was to have been established following electoral victory in 1852 were only too marked. Nevertheless, it was during the Second Republic, and in spite of the early onset of repression, that the idea of the Republic gained precision and mass support. Although substantial differences had appeared within the republican movement, between moderates and *démoc-socs*, to an important degree they still shared the universalistic ideals of the revolutionary years of 1789 to 1794. The insurrection of 1851, which in some respects had much in common with the archaic, 'primitive' traditions of popular protest, was inspired nevertheless by political ideology. *La République démocratique et sociale* had been presented, with some success, as the means of alleviating misery and insecurity and of creating a more just and egalitarian society. More broadly, the Second Republic represented an important stage in the process of mass politicisation. Historians have frequently associated politicisation with a vote for the left and against traditional social elites, but whether they voted for republican or conservative candidates large numbers of people, previously excluded from political activity, were now persuaded of its relevance to their daily lives. The introduction of manhood suffrage had stimulated political organisation and mobilisation. Doubtless, many soon relapsed into apathy, but others would continue to take at least an episodic interest in affairs outside their own communities. During the Second Empire the accelerating development of education, communications, urban reconstruction, regular (even if stage-managed) electoral campaigns, and the growing governmental intervention within communities which all this required, would reinforce these trends.

Towards an imperial restoration

Most of the population even in those regions in which resistance did occur had responded to news of the coup with indifference or delight. Among notables, initial reservations about the replacement of a liberal parliamentary regime by a Bonapartist military dictatorship were short lived. The acts of resistance to the coup were taken to confirm its necessity as a means of preventing a future socialist revolution. According to Morny (quoted in Dansett 1961: 366), the insurrections were clear evidence of the 'social war which would have broken out in 1852'. Grossly exaggerated accounts of *démoc-soc* atrocities (the murder and mutilation of gendarmes, pillage and rape) and presentation of the insurrections as a form of mindless violence (*jacquerie*) were used to heighten conservative fears. After long years of economic crisis and political ins͛ ͼ-bility, the promise of strong government proved to be attractive to r ͺ ͵ people. Whatever their political principles, monarchist notables rallied to the cause of social order (or at least remained silent). The Church gave thanks for deliverance with solemn *Te Deum*s. Salvation, in the short term at least, clearly lay in the hands of the police state. Even after the martial law which had been imposed in 32 departments ended on 27 March 1852, a complex of old and new laws facilitated administrative repression and effectively deterred political opposition. Lists of potential opponents were maintained in each department to facilitate further arrests should these be judged to be necessary. Detailed military contingency plans were prepared to deal with any future mass insurrections in Paris and Lyon. Censorship of the press and the surveillance of former militants and their likely meeting places continued. Control of the press was a major pre-occupation for the authorities, who blamed much of the disorder of the Second Republic on its corrupting influence. The new press law of 17 February 1852 codified the repressive legislation introduced since 1814 – prior authorisation preceding publication, the deposit of caution money to pay fines, stamp duty to increase the cost of newspapers, suspension, etc. – and increased the discretionary powers of the administration. Editors were obliged to engage in rigorous self-censorship if their newspapers were to survive. However, it proved to be easier to suppress opposition newspapers than to create a popular pro-government press. It should be noted, additionally, that respect for legal forms, an ethical code, lack of policemen and sheer inefficiency restricted the activities of the repressive apparatus. The police state of Louis-Napoléon Bonaparte, as brutal as it could be on occasion, was to be nothing like the twentieth-century totalitarian state. However, to an important degree, its origins in a military coup would determine attitudes towards the restored imperial regime and its subsequent evolution.

On 20 December 1851, a plebiscite was held on the question of extending the authority of the President of the Republic. This procedure was to be a characteristic of the new regime. Louis-Napoléon was determined to secure a large and positive majority. It was made clear to officials at all levels, from the prefect to the village mayor and road repair man that their continued employment depended upon enthusiastic campaigning. The essential theme was the choice between 'civilisation and barbarism, social order and chaos'. The promise was an end to the long mid-century crisis and the inauguration of an era of order, peace and prosperity. At the same time, every effort was made to intimidate opponents and to prevent them from campaigning. The result was predictable. A substantial positive majority was obtained, due in part to coercion but, primarily, because many voters were genuinely frightened at the prospect of further revolution, and large numbers were attracted by the prospect of a strong and active Bonapartist regime. About 7, 500, 000 voted 'yes'; 640, 000 'no'; and 1, 500, 000 abstained. A large negative vote was characteristic of all the major cities with 80, 000 'no' votes and 75, 000 abstentions countering only 132, 000 'yes' votes in Paris. In the Nord, significant opposition was expressed in Lille with its socio-professionally mixed population, but in the mining and metallurgical centres of Anzin and Denain, 79 per cent and 84 per cent respectively of the overwhelmingly working class electorate voted 'yes'. Two forms of opposition manifested themselves. A negative vote was returned, especially among the urban professional and lower middle classes, and skilled and literate workers in areas of republican strength in the north, east and south-east. Paradoxically, the exceptions in these areas were places in which insurrections had occurred. There, terrified conservatives voted 'yes' in gratitude to Bonaparte while republican sympathisers did the same to escape further repression. The other form of opposition was abstention, particularly evident in parts of the west and in Provence, where popular Legitimism and clericalism remained strong. Even then most Legitimists voted 'yes' (as did many former moderate republicans) and largely out of a concern for social order. The conservative newspaper, *L'Union bourguignonne* (16 December 1851), warned that 'those who vote NO declare themselves accomplices in the crimes of the demagogues'.

In symbolic promise of things to come, the plebiscite was followed by the replacement of the image of the Republic on coins and postage stamps by that of 'His Imperial Highness the Prince-President' as he was now to be officially designated. On 1 January 1852 at a solemn service of thanksgiving in Notre Dame, the Archbishop of Paris called for God's blessing on the regime using language which made it seem as if the Empire already existed and on 10 May new flags bearing the imperial eagle were distributed to the army. Relieved of their terror, the upper classes celebrated the carnival in 1852 with renewed enthusiasm. Within a year, following a similar, orchestrated campaign, a second plebiscite was held in far less dramatic circumstances (on 21–22 November 1852) with voters asked to approve the re-establishment of the hereditary empire. During a tour of the south in October, the future Emperor promised peace, order and prosperity. These themes, together with that of reconciliation, were taken up successfully by officials throughout the country. Again, open opposition was not tolerated. While 7, 824, 000 voters supported the proposed constitutional change, only 253, 000 voted against and 1, 500, 000 abstained – as before, mainly in the towns, in some 'red' areas of the south and in Legitimist dominated zones of the west. The Second Empire was proclaimed on 2 December 1852, a propitious date, the anniversary not only of Louis-Napoléon's own successful coup, but of both the coronation of his uncle in 1804 and the first Emperor's great victory at Austerlitz in 1805.

3

The authoritarian Empire

Objectives and achievements

The Second Empire would see major structural changes in the economy and society as well as innovations in the system of government. One of the fundamental questions to concern us will be the effect of these on political behaviour; another will be how to escape from the deforming prism of republican historiography. The intentions of Napoléon III, whose personal power had been greatly reinforced by the coup, were obviously of considerable significance. As we have seen, the reputation of this strange man, inspired by a belief in his own destiny, suffered irreparably from the catastrophic defeat of the French armies in 1870. However, he cannot be dismissed (as he was by some contemporaries) as 'Napoléon the Little' (Hugo). The objectives of the new Emperor, his Napoleonic ideas, were clear. He intended to de-politicise government through the establishment of a strong and stable executive power capable of promoting social and economic modernisa-tion and to 'close the era of revolution by satisfying the legitimate needs of the people'. The means to be employed included the restora-tion of the political and administrative institutions conceived by Napoléon I, together with severe curbs imposed upon the activities of political 'parties'. The Emperor, his authority legitimised by the popular vote, would serve as an almost mystical link between the state and society. Popular sovereignty would itself survive through the plebiscit-ory process and eventually, once social stability had been secured, through the gradual and partial re-establishment of parliamentary institutions. In the meantime, a senate made up of 180 senators was appointed, named for life, to include senior officials and military officers, representatives of the Church and of business, together with the imperial princes and various other dignitaries. Its role was, through the mechanism of the *senatus consultum*, to interpret and amend the constitution. It was also supposed to serve as the guardian of liberty by ensuring that laws were not introduced contrary to the constitution, to religion, morality, individual liberty and equality, to the sanctity of property and the security of France. In theory, the Senate then possessed considerable power; in practice, composed as it was of aged pensioners of the regime, it would do little to oppose the wishes of the government. Of far greater importance was the *Corps législatif*. With just over 260 members, elected by manhood suffrage, it had the right to vote on legislative and taxation proposals, but not to initiate legislation. Even during its most authoritarian phase the regime was never able to ignore entirely the opinions of a body, with potential power, made up of representatives of the social elite. Careful selection of candidates was thus seen as essential. The responsibility for actually drafting laws and administrative regulations, and for discussing amendments proposed by the *Corps législatif* rested with the 40 or 50 members, primarily jurists, of the Council of State (*Conseil d'Etat*). This, the supreme administrative tribunal, now received considerable political power, although it could be held in check with comparative ease by a government which was able to dismiss its members at will from their lucrative positions. Furthermore, its powers were resented bitterly by those whose legislative efforts it criticised – ministers, civil servants and deputies.

The regime was fortunate in that it coincided with a worldwide period of economic growth. Many of its 'achievements' might be regarded as simply coincidental. However, it would probably be more accurate to accept that the impact of trends in the international economy were reinforced internally by substantial government-inspired efforts to increase infrastructure investment, especially in roads, railways and the electric telegraph, as the means of achieving a transport 'revolution'. The railway network which had been composed of 3, 230 kilometres in discontinuous sections in 1851 had expanded to a network of 17, 200 kilometres by 1870. Furthermore, road links to railway stations had also been substantially improved. This, along with a marked reduction in tariff protection, secured through the negotiation of customs treaties with the country's main trading partners, beginning with Britain in 1860, was intended to ensure the development of more integrated and increasingly competitive markets for both agricultural and manufactured goods. The aim was to create a business environment conducive to investment in modern technology, with capital provided by new investment banks and investment facilitated by making it easier in law to establish joint stock companies with limited liability. Substantial capital was also to be mobilised in order to finance the creation of a capital city fit for the empire, with broad boulevards flanked by new commercial and residential buildings, allowing easy movement between the railway stations and facilitating, if necessary, the maintenance of military control through strategically placed barracks, fewer obstacles to cavalry charges and clear fields of fire for artillery. Similar (if less ambitious) developments graced most provincial cities. Along with enhanced opportunities for profit, it was hoped that large-scale investment would provide employment opportunities, greater security and improved rewards for the masses and, in so doing, contribute to the preservation of social stability. The objectives were clear, but economic and social modernisation takes time. Additionally, it was impossible to insulate the country against the vagaries of the international economic cycle or climatically induced harvest failures, as well as the confidence-sapping impact of international or internal political crises. As a result, these far-reaching economic and social objectives were attained only partially. Moreover, governmental intervention in economic affairs provoked considerable hostility from a variety of special interest groups; neither did it follow that the improved living conditions would automatically promote a greater sense of loyalty to the regime. Even so, the imperial years saw considerable progress in terms of economic modernisation and the improvement of living standards. This was symbolised by the virtual disappearance, as a consequence of market integration resulting from improved communications of the age-old subsistence crises, of the successive dearths which had caused so much misery and widespread popular protest as recently as 1845–7 and again in 1853–6. The continuing improvements in agricultural productivity as well as increased migration to the cities had the effect of easing population pressure on the resources of the countryside. In contrast with the long period of price depression from 1817 to 1851, the prices paid to farmers for their produce rose almost continuously in response to growing urban demand. However, if the various forms of farm income – profits, rents and wages – were all rising, this did not eliminate social tension in the countryside. Particularly in the 1860s, as the long established situation in which rising population densities had reinforced the power of the social elites who controlled access to scarce resources came towards an end, peasant farmers and even agricultural labourers clearly were developing a greater sense of independence. In the towns, too, the rapid growth of employment opportunities ensured that workers' real incomes began to rise from the late 1850s for the first time since the end of the First Empire. Although the living standards of the masses remained extremely poor by twentieth-century standards and harsh working and living conditions continued to result in widespread poor health, chronic insecurity and premature death, the Second Empire should still be seen as a period when the good years outnumbered the bad, when the France of Balzac was transformed into that described with equal literary brilliance by Emile Zola.

It was during the first decade, certainly until 1857, that the personal power of Napoléon III was at its peak. Ministers were convoked twice a week to discuss an agenda drawn up by the Emperor. They provided information, he took decisions. The tradition of ministerial responsibility to parliament (developed since 1814) was annulled and the *Corps législatif* rendered largely quiescent. These were years in which continued political repression and close cooperation with reactionary and clerical forces characterised the regime. Even during this period, however, implementation of governmental decisions was to be obstructed by a complex of often conflicting vested interest groups, as well as the practical difficulties of administrative control and finance, and by vacillation on the part of the head of state himself. Additionally, the new regime was dependent inescapably upon the aristocratic and wealthy *grands bourgeois* servants of previous regimes. Most ministers were conservative ex-Orleanists (e.g. Magne, Fould, Rouher) or representatives of the former dynastic opposition (Baroche). Of men who might be considered genuine Bonapartists, there were remarkably few. Napoléon's frustrations are said to have led to the exasperated comment: 'What a government is mine! The Empress is Legitimist; Napoléon-Jérôme republican; Morny Orleanist; I am myself a socialist. The only Bonapartist is Persigny and he is mad' (Plessis 1985: 54). Implementation of policy decisions depended upon the efficiency and goodwill of these men and of administrators drawn from similar backgrounds, and the Emperor was inevitably forced to make compromises.

The political system of Napoléon III

The power of an apparently monolithic, centralised, hierarchical administration was reduced substantially by a combination of vested interests, localism, established habits and respect for the rule of law. The linchpin of the system – the Prefect, responsible for the whole range of government activities at departmental level – was himself subject to complex pressures from ministers, deputies, competing administrative hierarchies, mayors and the local notables who gathered regularly on an informal basis, at agricultural shows and at meetings of chambers of commerce and of the departmental councils (*conseils généraux*). Dependent on their routine collaboration, especially during elections, the Prefect could not afford to ignore their wishes. The intention expressed by genuine Bonapartists, like the prefect of the Haute-Garonne Pietri in 1854, of replacing the patronage and influence of the old elites by that of the Prefect, as the direct representative of the Emperor himself, was rarely realised. To a substantial degree, prefects were assessed by their superiors according to their success in managing elections. Election campaigns were the means of mobilising support. Electoral victory was vitally important for a regime which insisted upon its roots in popular sovereignty. It was an essential source of legitimacy. Thus, every election took on a plebiscatory character and involved a judgement of the regime and its policies. This was not only the case in general elections, but also frequently those at departmental and municipal level, whenever the personality of the candidate or local circumstances gave the contest a political colouring. Until 1869, the essential distinguishing feature of the electoral system was the official candidature, far more systematically organised than under previous regimes. The government, through the agency of the Minister of the Interior and the prefects subordinate to him, took it upon itself to declare support for some candidates and to announce its hostility to others. Once selected, usually at the suggestion of the Prefect, the government's candidate could expect active support from the entire administrative machine by means of the creative re-drawing of constituency boundaries, the distribution of the official candidates ballot papers along with registration cards, and of oral and printed propaganda. Initially, this insisted upon the Emperor's role in protecting France from the 'red menace', and then from around 1857 used the theme of prosperity, the progress of public works (particularly roads and railways) and the efforts of the regime to attenuate the misery caused by poor harvests. At the same time, opponents were discriminated against. Their posters were torn down, the printers of opposition manifestos risked losing their all-important licenses, meetings were banned and potential candidates and their supporters were intimidated. Moderate opposition was tolerated, most notably in the republican and anti-clerical newspaper *Le Siècle*, and at the opposite pole in the ultramontane Catholic *Univers* edited by Louis Veuillot, but on condition that the regime itself was not challenged.

A major political problem, even in the 1850s, was the selection of official candidates. These needed to satisfy two main criteria – devotion to the regime and possession of the local influence necessary for electoral success, although it was always possible that an excess of local influence might allow deputies like the right-wing Bonapartist Granier de Cassagnac in the Gers to become too independent of the government. The number of suitably qualified candidates was generally limited. In practice, given the absence of a Bonapartist party, they were mainly former Orleanist or Legitimist notables. Additionally, the very act of selecting a particular individual was all too likely to cause disaffection among disappointed aspirants, with a cumulative effect over time. Thus, the authoritarian political system was always in danger of breaking down due to its inability to escape from dependence upon the established elites. Moreover, once these elites had recovered from their fear of 'red' revolution, they would demand the restitution of the share of political power they had enjoyed under the July Monarchy and the liberal institutions through which this could be manifested. As the former Orleanist prime minister Guizot warned:

> an insurrection can be repressed with soldiers; an election won with peasants. But the support of soldiers and peasants is not sufficient to rule. The cooperation of the upper classes who are naturally rulers is essential.

Napoléon appears to have hoped that the elites would genuinely rally to the new regime once its stability was assured. He was to be disappointed. Indeed, his very success in re-establishing social order would soon make the authoritarian regime appear redundant.

In the early years, political stability and strong government accompanied by growing economic prosperity certainly attracted considerable support. The Emperor was able to pose as the 'saviour of society'. Even Guizot had accepted that the regime was 'inevitable and necessary' (letter of 12 January 1852). In such diverse worlds as the relatively backward and overwhelmingly rural west with its Legitimist and clerical traditions, or the north with its advanced farming and rapidly developing industry, the mid-century crisis had reinforced the influence of local elites. They possessed multifaceted means of exercising social power, based upon control of access to the land, to employment and to the charity upon which so many people came to depend in a period of intense depression. However, they were willing to collaborate with an administration committed to protecting their status. Typically, in the department of the Nord, most politicians assumed that to do anything else would result in their political isolation, given the widespread appreciation of the improved economic and social situation of the 1850s. In the west and parts of the south, many Legitimist notables faced a sharp moral dilemma as a result of the re-establishment of the Empire. Traditional family loyalties could hardly be ignored. Most, however, were 'realists' and even if the majority did not rally with any real enthusiasm, their criticism of the new regime would, for some time, remain muted. In the Gard, for example, the spirit of cooperation was rewarded by the selection for the February 1852 elections of three Legitimists – the Duc d'Uzès and the Marquis de Calvières (with interests in both the land and industrial development) and the merchant Léonce Curnier – as official candidates. The clergy also assumed that their interests would be served best by maintaining a close alliance with a regime which appeared to want to encourage the extension of clerical influence in education and society as a whole, as a means of inculcating sound moral principles and safeguarding social order. This policy was given symbolic value through the attendance of government representatives at all public religious ceremonies, practical significance by means of increased stipends for priests, and substantial subsidies for church construction and repairs. For the government, this policy had the useful consequence of reducing the ability of the Legitimists, acting through the clergy, to speak to a mass audience. A much remarked upon manifestation of this weakening of popular Legitimism was provided by the enthusiastic reception given to the imperial couple by parish priests and their flocks during their visit to Brittany in 1858.

Mass electoral support for the regime was partly the result of official election management degenerating at times into coercion and the ability to make use of the social influence of local elites and of the clergy. In most departments, given the small number of bureaucrats, the government acted through the existing elites and inadvertently strengthened their local authority. Rarely was use made of the predominantly middle-class electoral committees which were set up in many areas. As a result, their members were soon discouraged. The opportunity to establish a committed Bonapartist party was missed. Napoléon himself, as well as his close advisors, were too closely integrated into 'high' society and committed to the established social order to be able to contemplate seriously the organisation of a 'party' as an alternative means of exercising influence. The brilliance of the imperial court at the Tuileries is evidence of a determination to reinforce these traditional links. This is, of course, in marked contrast to the party based systems of control introduced in Nazi Germany and Soviet Russia. In only a few areas, most notably former centres of *démoc-soc* strength in impoverished regions with relatively few resident notables (e.g. the Creuse or Basses-Alpes), was it judged possible to appeal to the egalitarian instincts of the masses over the heads of established elites and on the basis of such issues as restrictions on peasant access to forests and the burden of usury. Bonapartism in these limited contexts might be seen as a democratising movement, a means of reducing the power of the 'bigwigs' (*gros*) over the 'little people' (*petits*). However, the key factor in winning and retaining support for the regime in most rural areas, and for all social groups, was to be the establishment of strong and stable government and the greater prosperity which appeared to follow. Even if most of the rural population continued to take little interest in politics they were grateful for this, and also aware of the dependence of the regime on their vote. Napoléon III was 'their Emperor'.

Although the Emperor and officials at all levels frequently expressed sympathy for industrial workers, their limited efforts to alleviate working and living conditions had little practical impact, while the constant efforts to repress workers' organisations and strikes in order to safeguard the 'freedom' of economic activity were clearly favourable to employers. Even so, and although republican historiography has attempted to minimise its significance, many workers were also attracted by the regime, especially in the Nord, Rouen area and Alsace. In part, this was due to the Bonapartist legend and mass propaganda presenting Napoléon III as the 'poor man's friend'. Relative prosperity, in spite of some difficult years, lent weight to this, as did the efforts of the administration to alleviate the effects of poor harvests, rising food prices and unemployment between 1853 and 1857. It also reflected clerical influence in some of the declining textile centres in the south, or else paternalistic pressures, as among the employees of the textile entrepreneur Seydoux at Le Cateau (Nord) and those of the ironmasters Schneider at Le Creusot (Saône-et Loire) and de Wendel at Hayange (Moselle). The many workers employed in rural manufacture tended to share the views of the peasants among whom they lived. In addition, the waging of successful war was to be an important source of prestige for the regime. Even in such major centres of opposition as Paris and Lyons, events like the Emperor's departure for Italy with the army in 1859 appealed to a bellicose popular nationalism.

Foreign policy

Napoléon's foreign policy was that of the republican left of the time. It involved rejection of the treaties imposed on France in 1815 following the defeat of the first Empire and, even more ambitiously, a recasting of the map of Europe based on the principle of nationality, to involve in particular some sort of reconstitution of Poland, Italy and Germany as well as the territorial *aggrandisement* of France itself. As far as possible, these objectives were to be achieved through congresses of the powers but, if necessary, through engagement in limited war. The Crimean war in 1854 represented a first step, an alliance with Britain against Russia, the most reactionary of European states. Eventual military success considerably increased French prestige, although the Congress of Paris in 1856 did not result in revision of the treaties. War with the old rival Austria in 1859 brought further military successes at Magenta and Solferino in Northern Italy and a hastily concluded peace which united Lombardy to the Kingdom of Piedmont-Savoy and could not prevent Italian nationalists from seizing power in the duchies of Tuscany, Parma and Modena and in the Papal Romagna. As a reward, the territories of Savoy and Nice lost in 1815 were, following plebiscites of their inhabitants, triumphantly restored to France. Popular images and songs celebrated this renewal of national glory. The return of the Imperial Guard and other military units to Paris from the Crimea on 29 December 1855 and from Italy on 14 August 1859, still in their battle-torn uniforms, carrying their tattered flags, with gaps in their ranks left by the dead, attracted enormous emotional crowds. The Emperor's birthday on 15 August, celebrated as a national holiday, provided another opportunity for military parades in every garrison town in France. Patriotic enthusiasm there undoubtedly was, but reports from both prefects and state prosecutors (*procureurs-généraux*) also suggest that there were always substantial public misgivings about military adventure. The actual outbreak of war might be greeted with resigned acceptance, turning towards general support. However, as the Crimean war was prolonged, criticism revived and with it demands for a negotiated settlement. Similarly, during the Italian campaign, reports from the provinces following the victories at Magenta and Solferino reveal both a pride in French successes and widespread support for an immediate peace. Only committed republicans favoured the complete defeat of Austria. The government's constant concern with the state of public opinion and particular anxiety about alienating normal supporters among the elites, business circles and the rural population, ensured that these reports were taken into account in official discussions of foreign policy, although their impact on decisions is difficult to establish. The despatch of an expeditionary force to Mexico in December 1861 – 30, 000 men by the end of 1862 – in pursuit of the dream of creating a French sphere of influence in the Americas at a time when the USA was fully absorbed with civil war, would prove to be beyond the public's comprehension. It perfectly illustrated the danger, for a regime so constantly concerned with public opinion, of policy decisions which were difficult to justify as serving the nation's vital interests. Not surprisingly, just as foreign policy initiatives judged by the public to be successful considerably enhanced the regime's prestige, so failures could be extremely damaging.

Signs of dissent

During its first decade, the Second Empire enjoyed a broader consensus of support than its predecessors. Election results suggest that this reached its apogee in 1857 when official candidates obtained 89 per cent of the votes cast although, due to large-scale abstention, this represented only 60 per cent of registered voters. Even at this stage, however, prefects were increasingly anxious, especially about the cities in which supervision of the electorate was always so difficult. Much of the support for the regime, particularly from the elites, had always been conditional and far from wholehearted. It declined as the threat of a revolutionary upheaval diminished. The state prosecutor at Aix-en-Provence reported with regret, as early as 16 June 1855, that 'if the government has few really dangerous enemies, the number of genuinely serious adherents upon whom it could count in a critical situation appears extremely restrained'. With order apparently restored, social elites would gradually, and initially with great restraint, increase their pressure for greater influence over political decision-making and for the re-establishment of a representative, parliamentary regime, both on principle and as a means of protecting their special interests. The growing number of critics ranged from those who had initially welcomed the coup but who no longer saw the practical need for authoritarian government, to republicans who, for the most part, rejected the Empire and all its works.

In the first category were diverse 'liberals', the socially conservative proponents of parliamentary government and of greater liberty for the press and local government. They expressed restrained criticism in newspapers like the *Journal des Débats* (circulation 12, 800 in 1861) or the *Revue des Deux Mondes* (circulation 12, 400). They were also well represented among the official deputies elected to the *Corps législatif*. Although established political personalities like Thiers or Rémusat continued to play influential roles, at local level informal liberal leadership frequently appears to have been undergoing renewal. This was due to the withdrawal from public life of those who had been disillusioned by the experience of the Second Republic, to the rallying of many, especially former Orleanists, to the imperial regime and because of the emergence of younger men especially from those excluded from office by the system of official candidature – a new generation of 'outs'. The liberal revival of the 1860s was being prepared. Initially, the lead was given by Legitimists. Their criticism was frequently tolerated by the regime because as obvious conservatives they were not a threat to social order. Typically, theirs was an elite 'party' based upon personal relationships and voluntary associations rather than specific forms of political organisation. Although instructed by the Comte de Chambord, the Legitimist pretender, to abstain from politics, they were often too determined to take full advantage of their influence in local and national elections to adopt this purist stance. This was true both of landed elites in the west and south and, in an industrial department like the Nord, of notables like the textile entrepreneur Kolb-Bernard, the Vicomte Anatole de Melun and the Comte de Caulaincourt who presided over the charitable work of the major Catholic lay organisation, the *Société de Saint-Vincent de Paul*. The activities of this *Société* throughout France caused growing concern to the administration. It brought together regularly members of the Legitimist elite and provided them with the means of exercising a wider influence over both fellow members and the recipients of charitable assistance. Moreover, many of these Legitimist sympathisers continued to hold important public offices, again ignoring Chambord's instructions to resign because this would have affected their incomes, reduced them to a tedious idleness and resulted in a significant loss of influence. In practice, although they might in private pour scorn on the bad taste of the imperial court and might fail to attend receptions at the prefecture, they generally cooperated with the government, justifying this at least initially by their common concern with the defence of order. Increasingly, though, the basis of this opposition from the right – potential rather than real – was changing. In place of dynastic loyalty, greater emphasis was placed upon defence of the interests of religion and the values of a traditional, hierarchical, rural society, against the destructive and demoralising tendencies of modern urban-industrial civilisation. Until 1859, however, the Roman Catholic Church remained on good terms with the regime, limiting the Legitimists' ability to use the clergy as a means of appealing for mass support. Only the Emperor's military intervention in Italy and an outcome which was unfavourable to the interests of the Papacy and offensive to the ultramontane instincts of most of the clergy, revived the traditional clerico-legitimist alliance. Even then, the results in terms of popular support were to be disappointing. Most practising Catholics failed to appreciate the need to protect the Pope's temporal power, partly because of the declining influence of the clergy, but mainly due to the competing attractions of the regime and, to a lesser degree, of an increasingly anti-clerical republican opposition.

This Republican opposition remained weak throughout the 1850s and beyond. The process of politicisation undergone during the Second Republic had not lasted long enough in most regions to establish a permanent mass commitment to the republic. The intensification of repression, moreover, had led to the disappearance of republican newspapers and organisations. The context for political activity, so fundamentally altered in February 1848, once again had drastically changed. The general atmosphere, especially in areas in which insurrections had occurred in December 1851, was described by one senior official as of 'humble and universal submission to the regime'. Many former activists, knowing themselves to be marked men, chose prudent inactivity. Between 1852 and at least 1857, administrative reports from the provinces reveal a sentiment of security, in great contrast with their extremely alarmist nature prior to the *coup d'état*. Nevertheless, even in these dark days, republican militants continued, cautiously, to meet. Using the camouflage provided by a multiplicity of voluntary and leisure associations which recruited through co-option, gatherings in work places, bars and private homes continued to provide cover for political activity. Individual protest occurred through seditious shouts and placards, while funerals supplied an occasional opportunity for the public demonstration of local support. Even in the years of relative political quiescence, prefects and state prosecutors continued to make reports, usually quite unsubstantiated, concerning the existence of republican secret societies. In March 1853, for example, the existence of a network with 19, 000 members in southern France was posited; more real, but still not posing a very substantial threat, was *la Marianne*, an organisation discovered in March 1855 with members in working-class districts of Paris and its suburbs and in diverse departments including the Nièvre, Loire-et-Cher and Maine-et-Loire. The most radical activists, according to the scanty evidence of underground activity, from such diverse milieu as Lille, Limoges, Toulouse and Draguignon (Var), appear to have been generally workers who resented bitterly the timidity, pretensions and social conservatism of the usually bourgeois local leadership. Pamphlets by exiles like Felix Pyat and most notably Victor Hugo (whose *Napoléon le petit*, *Histoire d'un crime* and *Châtiments* set the tone for generations of republican historians) were smuggled across the frontiers without too much difficulty. Bianchi's *The Industrial Worker in a Religious and Conservative Society* (1855) was read avidly by workers in Lille, a city in which, as in Paris or Lyon, an old-established republican tradition was able to resist the blandishments of the new regime and the de-politicisation which occurred elsewhere. Generally, however, it appears as if during the inevitable and frequently rancorous post-mortem and reappraisal of objectives and tactics which took place in these years, most republican militants determined to avoid further recourse to violence.

In spite of continued repression, it seems likely that the number of committed republicans remained more numerous than before 1848. Embittered by failure and repression, they began the long process of restoring links with sympathisers and of combating the often very genuine attractions of the imperial regime. Little is known about who these militants were, although according to a police list of republican activists in Lille in 1855 41 per cent were artisans, shopkeepers and small merchants, 10 per cent were middle bourgeois small manufacturers, and the rest mainly textile workers (Ménager 1979: 404). By 1858, it seems that members of the liberal professions were also returning to political opposition. In small provincial towns landowners, professional men, tradesmen and artisans began again to use their personal influence to win over the masses. The republican movement remained socially diverse, although in comparison with the Second Republic peasant support had declined markedly. Nevertheless, the cadres necessary for the eventual re-emergence of the republican party had frequently remained in existence or were being reconstituted gradually. In July 1853, the police chief in a previously agitated town like Cuers (Var) complained that the *démoc-socs* had established a sort of counter-society which patronised its own cafés, shops and doctors. Occasionally, it would demonstrate its strength in local elections. This was even the case in some of the areas in which insurrections had occurred and in which repression had been especially intense, particularly since most of the militants who had been arrested benefited from a succession of amnesties. However, it was still sensible to be cautious. A harsh reminder of this and of the repressive capacity of the regime was provided by the general security law (*loi de sûreté générale*) hurriedly introduced on 27 February 1858 following the attempt on 14 January 1858 by the Italian nationalist Orsini to assassinate the Emperor. Under its terms, 2, 883 republican suspects selected from the lists kept in every department were detained without trial, and some 350–400 deported to Algeria (Wright 1969: 416). However, the republican revival was interrupted only briefly by these measures which were followed indeed by a general amnesty on 16 August 1859. This act of clemency revealed that the government itself appreciated that exceptional measures of repression had become unacceptable to the general public, at least in the absence of a credible threat of revolution.

As an electoral force, the republican party had almost disappeared. In the 1852 elections committed republicans generally either voted for non-official conservative candidates or abstained. In Paris, the moderate republicans General Cavaignac and Hippolyte Carnot were elected and, in Lyons, Jacques Hénon. All three refused to take the oath of allegiance to the Emperor and were unseated. However, for other activists repeated elections at local, departmental and national levels proved to be too much of a temptation. Although in most areas the combination of administrative repression and the organisational problems faced by opposition groups ensured that successes were limited, electoral activity contributed to the gradual process of revival. In spite of the fact that in most departments organised electoral committees were not re-introduced before 1863 or even 1868, the signs of republican resurgence were evident much sooner. In the 1857 general elections, 100 candidates presented themselves (in 261 constituencies as a result of multiple candidacies), five were successful in Paris (Carnot, Goudchaux, Cavaignac, Ollivier and Darimon) and one in Lyons (Hénon). The refusal of Carnot to take the oath of allegiance and the death of Cavaignac, were followed by renewed victories in the ensuing by-elections, with the election of Jules Favre and Ernest Picard. Substantial support for the republican cause was also evident in other large cities, in spite of the restrictions placed upon opposition electioneering. For the urban *classes populaires*, the republic clearly remained the ideal form of government. However, these successes also revealed the continued strength of divisions within the republican movement. There was clearly a gulf between the more intransigent who claimed that abstention was the only principled policy and those, frequently representatives of the younger generation, like Ollivier and Darimon who were less rigid in their attitudes. Equally evident was the division which had caused so much strife in 1848 between the moderates, including all the elected deputies who were essentially democratic liberals committed to political change, and the radical and socialist advocates of social reform.

4

Liberalisation

From 1860 the context for political activity was again to be gradually transformed. Although, contrary to the periodisation commonly employed by historians, it is difficult to agree that a genuinely 'liberal' empire existed before May 1869 when most of the restrictions on the right to hold public meetings as well as on the press were finally lifted, significant steps had already been taken towards the creation of a parliamentary regime. A decree on 24 November 1860 conceded to the *Corps législatif* the right to discuss the address from the throne outlining government policy at the beginning of each parliamentary session. The Emperor further announced his attention to nominate ministers without portfolio (initially Magne, Billault and Baroche) and, in 1863, a minister of state (Billault then Rouher) to explain and defend government policy before parliament. Moreover, parliamentary debates were now to be reproduced in full in the official *Moniteur* and might be reprinted in other newspapers. Publicity would provide the essential stimulus to debate. In December 1861, the Emperor responded to anxiety in conservative financial circles about the growth of the national debt and the unconventional arrangements made by Haussmann, as Prefect of the department of the Seine, for financing the massive public works programme which was transforming the capital. He conceded greater parliamentary control over the budget. This would provide the essential means for the extension of parliamentary influence in every sphere of policy. Throughout the decade too, although repressive legislation remained intact, much greater tolerance was displayed towards the press and public meetings, partly because of the adverse public reaction to the *loi de sûreté générale*. The introduction of more permissive legislation in 1868 would be seen by conservatives as the final opening of the flood gates.

Reasons for liberalisation

Why did this process of liberalisation occur? It seems likely that once social order had been secured, the Emperor had always intended to proceed with measures of reconciliation directed at liberals and republicans. He was encouraged in this, to varying degrees, by his half-brother Morny and by his cousins Walewski – the illegitimate son of Napoléon I – and the Prince Napoléon-Jérôme and he chose to ignore the misgivings of his more authoritarian ministers – Baroche, Fould and Rouher. He was anxious, given his own deteriorating health and the youth of his heir, the Prince-Imperial (born in 1856), to create a regime less dependent upon his own survival. It seems likely that he also realised that authoritarian government was becoming an obstacle to the maintenance of the business confidence so vital to the achievement of the economic and social modernisation he believed were essential both to internal stabilisation and the retention of France's great power status. Initially, at least, liberalisation probably represented confidence in the strength and stability of the regime and in its ability to control the process of change. However, the diverse series of ambitious decisions taken from 1859 and affecting both internal and foreign policy had complex and often contradictory effects. These included an amnesty for republicans; alliance with Piedmont-Savoy in support of a 'Europe of the nationalities' and as a further stage in the rejection of the humiliating peace imposed on France at Vienna in 1815; a loosening of the alliance between church and state established during the Second Republic in reaction against rampant clericalism; the pathbreaking 1860 commercial treaty with Britain and subsequently with other major trading partners which substantially reduced tariff protection, as a means of intensifying competitive pressures and forcing the pace of modernisation, of opening up new markets, and of improving diplomatic relations with Britain; the growing role accorded to the *Corps législatif*; and the legalisation of strikes in 1864. The sense of grievance aroused by these policies among a wide range of social groups, together with the growing awareness that the regime was unlikely again to resort to brute force against its opponents, encouraged increasingly open and vocal criticism, especially from those clericals and liberals who were reminded by the Italian and free trade policies that the Emperor was capable of using his prerogative powers to develop personal policies which might damage their own particular interests. Thus, they were encouraged to demand even greater parliamentary control over policy and a range of political reforms intended to increase their own influence.

The growing vitality of this liberal opposition, and increasingly also of the republicans, soon made it clear that the Emperor had failed to achieve his objective of securing some sort of national reconciliation. In this situation, Napoléon III, unlike his predecessors, was prepared to adapt. Liberalisation became primarily a means of assuring the elites upon whose cooperation the regime inescapably depended, by means of the restoration of at least some of the political power they had possessed during the July Monarchy. The prolonged and apparently grudging character of the process, however, would ensure that these socially conservative liberals would be less grateful than they might otherwise have been. Management of the process by which an authoritarian regime liberalised itself was fraught with all manner of difficulties. Once expectations had been aroused it would prove increasingly difficult to satisfy them. The Emperor's motives were always suspect. Certainly considerable suspicion would be aroused by his openings to the left. These involved conciliatory overtures to workers initiated by a discussion group established in the Palais Royale in Paris in 1861 by the 'republican' prince, Napoléon-Jérôme; the dispatch of a workers' delegation to the 1862 London International Exposition; the legalisation of strikes in 1864 which was combined with the growing toleration of technically illegal workers' organisations; and the ending of the inequality enshrined in legislation which had accepted the employers' word in preference to the workers' in case of dispute. Ultimately, this attempt to reduce the regime's dependence on the old elites failed. It could never have had more than a marginal impact on the conduct of government even if it had succeeded in reinforcing the regime's electoral strength. In practice, there was little alternative to the continued dependence on the traditional conservative and liberal political elites. In consequence, as support from all quarters declined, liberalisation increasingly came to represent a response to pressure. It constituted a sort of holding action against the apparently unending growth of opposition.

The growth of opposition

This growth was clearly evident in the gradual collapse of the system of official candidature beginning during the 1863 election campaign. The system was challenged in the first place by the simple increase in the number of opposition candidates and, consequently, in the scale of electoral agitation, and by the willingness of some former official candidates with powerful local bases to criticise government policy, even if this meant the loss of the administration's support in elections. Influential figures like the Marquises d'Andelarre and de Gramont, both of them landowners and deputies for the Haute-Saône, together with the textile entrepreneur Kolb-Bernard from the Nord and 45 other clerical and protectionist deputies, expressed their concern about the consequences of the Emperor's Italian policy for the temporal power and spiritual independence of the Papacy and of his free-trade policies for cereal prices and the viability of the metallurgical and textiles industries. Threateningly, in industrial centres like Reims and Saint-Etienne, it was not the established mercantile elite but the younger up-and-coming generation of businessmen, impatient at their exclusion from political power, who supported the liberal opposition, and who would provide by 1868–69 the funds required to establish newspapers like the Saint-Etienne *L'Eclaireur* and *L'Indépendence Rémois*. Significantly too, the political outlook of Orleanists of the older generation was evolving during the 1860s towards a liberalism more compatible with the system of manhood suffrage.

As elite commitment to the regime declined, effective electoral management became increasingly difficult. Reports from prefects and state prosecutors revealed that resentment of official interference with the 'dignity' and 'independence' of voters was accumulating. Even by many government supporters the full range of official pressure was felt to have become outmoded since the threat of revolution seemed to have disappeared. There appeared to be a growing risk that official advice to the electorate might simply be rejected, which inevitably called the whole system into question. In 1863, prefects had already begun to behave with noticeably greater circumspection, particularly in departments like the Nord in which so many notables already had been alienated by the regime's economic, foreign and religious policies. The call for the defence of vital local interests was a powerful means of reinforcing the influence of regional elites. In most parts of northern and central France, the majority of textile, metallurgical and mining entrepreneurs opposed the reduction in customs tariffs, exaggerated the likely impact of British competition, and mobilised substantial support through professional organisations, chambers of commerce, elected councils and the local press. From 1861 these views were represented in the *Corps législatif* by the influential deputies Kolb-Bernard, Plichon and Brame as well as by Thiers acting as the paid spokesman of the Anzin mining company. They tended to blame almost every economic ill upon the commercial treaty with Britain, despite the vagaries of the economic cycle and the disruptive impact of the American Civil War on the textiles and export industries. Additional targets were excessive government expenditure on the army and upon the embellishment of Paris and other cities, and such overseas adventures as the attempt to create a client state under the rule of the Habsburg Archduke Maximillian in Mexico. In the 1860s, Thiers once again assumed the role of the most effective parliamentary critic of the regime.

The results of the May 1863 elections registered the growth of opposition. Aware of their continued relative weakness, in some circumstances opposition groups were prepared to collaborate – a factor contributing to the election of eight republicans and Thiers in Paris and to that of the moderate republican Marie together with the eminent Legitimist lawyer Berryer in Marseille. However, such cooperation between extremes was talked about more often than effected. Of much greater significance was the tendency in constituencies where only one opposition candidate stood for opponents of the regime to concentrate their votes on him. Significantly, once the results were known, Persigny – a symbol of the authoritarian approach and responsible for the conduct of the elections as Minister of the Interior – was dismissed. Another consequence was the formation of an extremely heterogeneous parliamentary opposition which included some of the growing number of Legitimists prepared to ignore the Comte de Chambord's injunctions to abstain, irreconcilable Orleanist notables like Rémusat and Auguste Casimir-Perier, independent liberals and moderate republicans. In the short term, the most significant development was to be the emergence of a Third Party (*tiers parti*) made up of both monarchist and Bonapartist proponents of conservative, liberal reform. Although only 32 advocates of outright opposition to the regime had been successful (including 17 republicans and democratic liberals and 15 independents, i.e. conservative and essentially monarchist liberals and clericals), the fact that most large towns and, above all, Paris, the capital city of the Empire, had supported them was cause for considerable alarm. Moreover, if in most areas republican intervention had been rather tentative, the increasingly open and widespread expression of republican ideals gave considerable encouragement to still hesitant potential supporters.

By 1869, when general elections were again due, even those candidates still prepared to accept the official nomination regarded the most blatant forms of administrative pressure as counter-productive. There seemed to be a clear incompatibility between the system of official candidature and the liberties accorded to the press and public meetings so recently in 1868. Once again these reforms had decisively transformed the political context. Acts of political opposition had become far less risky than before. Moreover, an expansive economic and social environment had widened horizons and increased the sense of independence of many voters. Interest in politics was being renewed, ending the widespread indifference and apathy of the previous two decades. There was an immediate and spectacular revival in the number of newspapers and political meetings. The press law was especially important in the provinces where around 150 new newspapers were created in time for the 1869 election, with 120 of them hostile to the government (Zeldin 1958: 95). The maintenance of administrative surveillance and the slowness with which these reforms (promised in January 1867) were implemented as a result of the Emperor's unwillingness to break with loyal authoritarians like Rouher, Baroche and Persigny, once again made them appear to be a grudging response to pressure. In reaction to this hesitation in Paris and in 46 constituencies, the candidates favoured by the government refused, or were advised by the administration not to accept, the official designation. Furthermore, most of those who did accept the label felt obliged to distance themselves from the administration as well as to announce their support for the further extension of political liberties. The administration was certainly active in the election campaign, but far more discretely than ever before. Most prefects encouraged their candidates to become more self-reliant by establishing their own electoral committees and newspapers. This election, with its mass circulation newspapers of all political hues and its public meetings, was fought in an entirely different atmosphere from its predecessors. Moreover, in large part due to political uncertainty, the economic situation had remained depressed since 1865. The results were a severe blow to the regime. If they are compared with the results of previous elections the rise of opposition and the deterioration of the government's position become clear (see Table 4.1).

In total, 216 government supporters were elected, of whom only 180 were official candidates and 98 were government liberals whose views differed little from those of opposition liberals. The precipitant

Table 4.1 Legislative election results

	Registered voters	Votes for government	Votes for opposition	Abstentions
1852	9,836,000	5,248,000	810,000	3,613,000
1857	9,490,000	5,471,000	665,000	3,372,000
1863	9,938,000	5,308,000	1,954,000	2,714,000
1869	10,417,000	4,438,000	3,355,000	2,291,000

decline in support for the government among the local elites who provided the vast majority of election candidates meant that it was now often forced to support men who appeared to be the least-bad alternative. Seventy-eight declared opponents of the regime were elected (49 liberals and 29 republicans), and although of these only the more radical republicans appear to have been irrevocably opposed to the Empire as such, for the government, controlling the *Corps législatif* clearly was going to be extremely difficult. The results in Paris in particular had exceeded all opposition hopes, with 234,000 votes for their candidates against 77,000 for official candidates and 76,500 abstentions. It was the success of the republican candidates in the capital and the mass demonstrations of hostility to the regime which followed, on successive nights between 9 and 12 June, which especially impressed contemporaries. Crowds demonstrated by singing the banned *Marseillaise*, shouting *Vive la République* and smashing windows, and inevitably clashed with the police and cavalry called out to restore order. Some 500 arrests were made.

The rise of Republicanism

These developments, together with the belief that the final collapse of the imperial regime was inevitable and possibly their own political sympathies, have led many historians to exaggerate the strength of republican opposition. The results of the 1869 elections, if they say something about the support for avowed republicans, also suggest that there were definite limits to this. Moreover, it is not enough to explain these limits in terms of electoral manipulation by the regime or the political ignorance of the rural population – another old favourite. The precise nature of support for republicanism and the impact this might have had on wider political relationships need to be examined. The 1860s certainly had seen a considerable recovery from the depths of the early 1850s. With liberalisation, more of the militants of 1848 had re-entered the fray. Even though their ranks had been considerably depleted by death, men whose reputations had been made during the struggles of the Second Republic like Bianchi and Testelain in Lille, and often too the family members who shared their reputations, continued to assume key leadership roles. In Lille in 1870, one-third of the militants considered by the police to be dangerous were of the generation of 1848, and their influence was substantially greater than this proportion would suggest. The social tension generated in rapidly developing industrial centres perhaps explains the militancy of many Lille political activists. In most provincial centres, as in Dijon, moderate bourgeois leaders, often from the professions and belonging to masonic lodges, appear to have dominated republican politics, although more radical and less solidly middle-class elements were pressing them hard by 1869. Apparently, this was a national trend and can be seen in the challenge to moderates of the older generation like Jules Favre, Hippolyte Carnot and Ernest Picard – men who had retained the vague religiosity of 1848 and who condemned violence and class conflict – coming from younger radicals like Gambetta, Allain-Targé and Vermorel whose formative experiences had been different and who were far more aggressive in their hostility to the regime, in their anti-clericalism and their demands for a measure of social reform.

The activities of these political leaders, from around 1863, were designed to restore their influence among former republican militants, as a prelude to the extension of organisation and agitation among the previously largely uninvolved younger generations. Much of the activity was localised and directed at winning urban municipal power. This was easier than might appear at first glance. The constituencies for municipal elections generally differed from those for general elections, in that their boundaries had not been drawn in order to submerge the suspect urban electorate in a mass of rural voters. Thus, it was possible to win control or establish a significant presence on a substantial number of town councils and use this as a base for wider political activity. At Auch (Gers) in 1865, two barristers, two notaries, a solicitor, a doctor, a merchant, a landowner and a banker were elected as republicans (Palmade 1961: 93). Republicans gained control of the Toulouse city council in 1866, and although the council was dissolved and replaced by a nominated commission after a period of tense relations with the local prefect, even this outcome had considerable propaganda value. However, success was not without its problems. Thus, it soon became clear that there was a very real danger that opposition might be moderated or even turned into collaboration once councillors had been integrated into the broader administrative system. Practical problem solving replaced political combat. The process of gaining republican converts could also be frustratingly slow – inevitably so given that past experience of repression made many potential sympathisers cautious. Nevertheless, a growing awareness of what was possible developed, particularly once the 1868 laws had enlarged the scope for legal political activity. As we have seen, this increased participation in opposition politics, particularly in Paris, was sufficient to cause a crisis of confidence in the future stability of the regime.

The organisational basis for republican activity, as it slowly developed, took much the same forms as in 1848, with the establishment of *ad hoc* electoral committees, made up mainly of professionals and businessmen, to select and then support candidates. These were frequently associated with local newspapers which performed crucial coordinating functions and with the politicisation of a complex of voluntary associations ranging from the predominantly lower and middle-class masonic lodges and *cercles*, the artisanal mutual aid societies to the more popular cafés and popular drinking clubs – the *chambrées*. During the electoral campaigns of 1869–70, these informal structures were supplemented by the organisation of specifically political meetings. There was a trend, moreover, as interest in public affairs intensified for temporary, informal and leisure organisations to become more political and permanent. Nationally, the republican 'party' suffered until 1868 from the lack of an obvious leader, although visits by peripatetic opposition deputies like Simon, Pelletan or Favre helped to establish some sort of national coordination and encouraged local groups to feel that they were part of a larger movement. In that year, however, Gambetta achieved fame through his condemnation of the regime in highly publicised speeches made while serving as a defence lawyer in a series of political trials. In 1869, standing for election at Belleville, a working class district of Paris, and significantly against the veteran moderate republican Carnot, his programme with its vague promises of social reform was taken up by most of the republican press. This confirmed his ascendancy.

The forms and content of republican propaganda inevitably changed in response to political liberalisation. They became less dependent upon the illegal distribution of tracts and upon the oral circulation of information, although both remained important, and more upon the newspaper press. The diffusion of propaganda was made much easier. Numerous provincial newspapers were established – even if they frequently disappeared because of lack of support and financial difficulties. Moreover, the

Parisian press circulated far more widely throughout France due to the railways. It now included such overtly revolutionary newspapers as Rochefort's *La Lanterne* (May 1868) and its successor *La Marseillaise* (December 1869), Delescluze's *Le Réveil* ('The Awakening' – July 1868) and Victor Hugo's *Le Rappel* ('The Reminder'). One feature of their attacks on the regime was condemnation of its origins in a *coup d'état*. Republicans were able to use the ammunition provided by the journalist Eugene Ténot whose damning accounts of the brutality involved – in *Paris en décembre* and *La Province en décembre* – attracted widespread interest. Such a regime, according to the *Indépendent du Midi* (1 January 1869), might accord '*liberties* but never genuine *liberté*'. In contrast, a republican alternative was presented based upon interpretations of the *Declarations of the Rights of Man*, revised since the 1840s to take account of manhood suffrage and the need for social reform.

Another feature of this propaganda was its often virulent anti-clericalism: an outpouring of the hatred accumulated in reaction to two decades of militant and politically reactionary clericalism. This was one of the themes of the well-attended public meetings organised in the popular quarters of Paris. In these, and in spite of the obligatory presence of a police *commissaire*, all the doctrines of the clubs of 1848 were re-iterated. Yet, although it was the most extreme revolutionary meetings and newspapers which made the greatest impression on public opinion, most republican papers and gatherings were more moderate. They desperately sought to avoid identification with the threat of violent revolution. Instead, they pressed for continued political reform, confident that the free working of a system of manhood suffrage must inevitably lead to eventual electoral victory. Beyond this, they held out hope of social justice. In this respect, radicals like Gambetta promised tax reductions following cuts in wasteful government expenditure, the introduction of free and secular primary education and, in even vaguer terms, an improvement in the lot of the poor. It was these particular proposals which distinguished them from both the moderate republicans and socialists. Writing early in 1870, Gambetta typified a determination to attract support from all social groups and to avoid social conflict:

> we must re-state ... that for us the victory of democracy with its free institutions means security and prosperity for material interests, everybody's rights guaranteed, respect for property, protection of the legitimate and basic rights of labourers, the raising up morally and materially of the lower classes, but without compromising the posi-

tion of those favoured by wealth and talent. . . . Our single goal is to bring forth justice and social peace.

(Gambetta, *Indépendent du Midi*, 19 May 1869)

Most bourgeois republicans, even if aware of the need to promise social reform in order to win over the mass electorate, remained totally committed to the interests of private property and a liberal economic system. Furthermore, they were desperately anxious not to frighten the large numbers of small property owners, artisans and peasants. Their fundamental commitment was to 'progress without revolution'.

Although there was considerable overlap between radicals and socialists, the former appear to have been less committed to social reform than their predecessors, the *démoc-socs* of 1849–51. Moreover, they were always afraid of losing control over the urban masses who provided them with the bulk of their popular support. Ideologically, the lines of division between radicals and socialists were clearer than they had been during the Second Republic. There were few disciples of utopian socialism left by the late 1860s, although among artisans cooperative aspirations remained influential. In Paris, the most prominent spokesmen for a complex of revolutionary and socialist ideas were the disciples, mostly intellectuals and students, of Louis-Auguste Blanqui ('Blanquists'), proponents of a violent seizure of power by revolutionary secret societies, together with the far less extreme and largely working-class members of the Workers' International. The latter was founded in London in 1864 and initially tolerated by a government which welcomed its moderation and mutualism. Toleration wore thin when, in 1867, its members sought to support strikers and became involved in political demonstrations. Reports which grossly exaggerated its membership increased official alarm. In reality, with a nominal membership of around 30, 000 nationally at its peak early in 1870, its influence was limited outside Paris, Lyon, Rouen and Marseille (Rougerie 1964: 112). Its main impact was to add to conservative and to moderate republican fears of a red revolution, already heightened by the virulence of the left's propaganda and especially by the ways in which this was reported in the conservative press.

Paradoxically, most politically conscious workers, while suspicious of the motives of the bourgeois republicans, continued to vote for radical electoral candidates like Gambetta. The desire for working-class political autonomy was very much a minority phenomenon. In 1864, when three worker candidates – Blanc, Coutant and Tolain – had stood for election in Paris in support of social reform, they had been bitterly attacked by established republican politicians and accused of being Bonapartists. They obtained 342, 11 and 500 votes, respectively. Clearly, working-class militants still lacked political authority within their own class. It was to middle-class politicians that workers looked to satisfy their aspirations for greater equality and dignity. Far more widespread than adherence to any ideological position in the working-class quarters of Paris was a diffuse sense of injustice which could certainly awaken sympathy for demands for revolutionary change among the large crowds attending political meetings during 1869–70. Speakers who denounced the bourgeoisie for 'living off the sweat of the people' as vampires devouring 'those who work' and who condemned those who had 'assassinated' the people in June 1848 and the despotism established by the 'crime of December 1851', were warmly applauded. Many speakers looked forward to an imminent revolution which would allow a settling of accounts and 'the emancipation of the workers'. Nevertheless, it is difficult to judge to what degree this hostility towards employers and a repressive government, evident in the strike waves of the late 1860s, was translated into a desire for revolutionary change. In general , it seems that, although many among the younger generations of worker militants rejected the utopian socialism of their fathers' generation in favour of collectivism and syndicalism, the widespread desire for social reform was successfully channelled by republican politicians into a vague reformism redolent of February 1848.

The republican movement, united in opposition to the Empire and on the principle of popular sovereignty, was otherwise bitterly divided over questions of personality, tactics and principle. For most of its leaders, winning over and then retaining mass support was the major objective. Socialism was seen as a threat to this and to the liberal economic and social principles to which both moderate and radical politicians alike subscribed. They rejected forcefully what they regarded as the extremist propaganda of the left, which by its re-creation of the 'red spectre' threatened to frighten the electorate and to alienate in particular the property-owning lower middle classes and peasants. In addition, they were afraid that it would provoke a repressive government response. Moderate republicans like Favre, Carnot, Simon and Picard, accustomed to working within the institutions of the Second Empire, seem to have been willing to rely entirely upon legal, parliamentary methods of securing concessions into the indefinite future, insisting upon their commitment to social order and arousing suspicion that they too, like Ollivier and Darimon, might eventually rally to the regime. These *hommes de 1848*, who had failed once already, were criticised by younger men like Gambetta, Spuller, Allain-Targé and Vermorel. The latter also opposed the violent rhetoric of revolutionaries such as the influential journalist Rochefort, and future leaders of the Paris Commune in 1871 such as the Blanquist Raoul Rigault and the neo-Jacobin Delescluze, both committed to the organisation of a revolutionary coup. Relationships between these republican factions were extremely poor and in the 1869 elections in Paris and Lyon, republicans would stand against each other for election.

Support for the republicans cannot be defined easily. It was present in all social groups, but was particularly strong in urban centres, in both the major cities and numerous small towns like Beaune, Gevrey or Nolay in the Côte d'Or, for example, where little groups of activists had been at work since the 1830s. In part, it was the product of the continuing competition for local power between established elites and up-and-coming bourgeois groups. In the industrial centres of Reims and Saint-Etienne, this occurred between the old-established merchant capitalists and the more enterprising among the new manufacturers and members of the liberal professions. These men were prepared to finance newspapers, organise committees, select candidates from within their own ranks and offer leadership, and generally to encourage the diffusion of democratic ideas through the network of workshops, cafés and mutual aid societies. Urban workers also increasingly came to support republican electoral candidates. Even if every manifestation of discontent, such as the strike waves of 1869–70, should not necessarily be taken to represent opposition to the regime, as opposed to support for professional demands or a protest against the rising cost of living, support for republicanism tended to be generated by such conflict which frequently brought strikers up against the legal and military representatives of the regime. Although living standards undoubtedly had improved for most workers during the late 1850s and 1860s, they remained more aware of cramped and often squalid housing, rising rents, and constant insecurity of employment, with even the most highly skilled conscious of the intensifying threat to their craft skills and status as industrial mechanisation and the re-organisation of work processes continued. Perceptions matter far more than realities in determining political behaviour.

The rural vote

The rural population as a whole was much less likely to vote for republican candidates. Any exercise in historical political sociology is, however, difficult. Generalisations are hazardous in the extreme. A complex of factors ensured that particular regions adopted one form of political identity or another. These included existing social relationships, the products of daily social intercourse, as well as the formative influence of memories of past conflict during the *ancien régime* and the revolution, and more recently during the Second Republic. The development of regular and intensifying links with urban centres and especially with the artisans and professional men resident in the small market centres, as well as factors such as levels of literacy, the forms of habitat structure and established patterns of popular sociability, were other relevant factors facilitating or obstructing the diffusion of ideas and political organisation. The regions of northern France with the most advanced agriculture, prosperous farms and social systems closely controlled by large-scale commercial and mainly tenant farmers, and from which the most disaffected could migrate with relative ease, tended to support official candidates. In the east, in the Côte d'Or studied in such detail by Lévêque (1983), both the Châtillonais (a society dominated by peasant landowners and where social tension was limited) and the Brionnais (in which large landowners in close alliance with the clergy were dominant) voted for the regime. In contrast, it was the areas of vine cultivation and of predominantly cereal-producing plains around Châlons and Dijon – open societies engaged in commerce, subject to the alcohol tax and intensifying competitive pressures and especially susceptible to outside influences – which provided substantial support for republicans. Indeed, this usually appears to have been found in areas in which commercial farming and rural manufacture coexisted as well as in places of passage, in the east of Côte d'Or, the south of Doubs, Northern Jura, along the Rhône-Saône corridor and in the coastal regions of Provence and Languedoc and in the Garonne valley. In all these places, strong republican minorities existed by 1869. In the Limousin, cantons susceptible to Parisian influence because of the practice of migratory labour began to record 20–30 per cent support for republican candidates (Corbin 1975). In the central Morvan, republican ideas re-surfaced in areas isolated by poor communications and dispersed habitat which might have been expected to have remained loyal to the right. In practice, it proved difficult for the administration to dominate an impoverished peasantry which had been alienated by the efforts of largely absentee landowners to restrict traditional rights of usage in the forests – a vital part of traditional pastoral farming systems (Vigreux 1987). In a variety of situations, the rural population might therefore be attracted to the republican cause.

Surprisingly, republican militants made relatively little effort to appeal specifically to the rural population, although of course it made up a majority of the electorate. Newspapers like the *Rappel de la Provence* (1869) – with its low price and short and simply written articles designed to appeal to the practical concerns of the habitués of the *chambrées* of the Var – were rare. In attempting to appeal to peasants, republicans developed programmes similar to, but in many respects less radical than, those of the *démoc-socs* in 1849. The condemnation of wasteful government expenditure and high taxes was retained and attacks on the regime's military adventures and the growing burden of conscription were added. Significantly, the more radical promise of cheap credit to allow peasants to purchase land had all but disappeared. Nevertheless, on this basis republicans were able to attract some support, especially in those areas in which a republican tradition had previously been established during the Second Republic or before, although on this occasion in the south-east rather than the centre and south-west, and nowhere on the same scale. Indeed, in some areas support seems to have melted away in the intervening years. In the Limousin, most notably, continued hostility towards traditional elites was combined now with support for the 'Emperor of the Peasants and Masons' who had brought prosperity to the countryside and work for those who depended on temporary migration to the burgeoning building sites of Paris and Lyon. In departments as diverse as the Basses-Alpes and Gers which had experienced large-scale insurrections in resistance to the coup d'état in 1851, the official candidates would be re-elected easily in 1869. Virtually the whole south-west in fact appears to have been won over to the regime. In a large number of departments there was almost no mass support for the opposition. Pessimistically, the liberal Prévost-Paradol described the regime as 'an Imperial ruralocracy' based upon 'rural imbecility and provincial bestiality', a view shared by the republican Allain-Targé who stressed the need for the future republic to educate the 'thirty-five million brutes who compose the Nation to the rank of active citizens'. Republicans habitually explained election defeat in terms of pressure from the administration, traditional elites and the clergy, combined with the sheer ignorance and susceptibility of the rural masses. It rarely seems to have been admitted that support for the Empire might represent a rational decision in favour of a regime which had brought order and prosperity. This option was reinforced by the conservative propaganda which sought to re-create the threat from the so-called *partageux*, the communists who supposedly intended to seize the land. In the Paris basin, the west, north and much of the south-west, socially dominant landowners and large farmers, supported by the clergy, stimulated these fears. Thus, in the village of Moux in the Morvan, the mayor reminded the electorate that to vote for a republican candidate meant 'a vote for revolution, for the red flag, for the guillotine'.

Establishment of the liberal Empire

If the regime had retained the bulk of its rural support, the results of the 1869 elections nevertheless revealed the accelerating deterioration in its position and the growing risk of isolation. A total of 116 deputies drawn from both the opposition and government liberals combined to demand a ministry responsible to the *Corps législatif*. Concessions urgently needed to be made if support for the regime among the social and political elites was to be maintained. It was therefore decided by the Emperor that parliament should be allowed much wider rights in the questioning of ministers and control of the budget. As a result, effective administration would depend in future on the ability of ministers to secure the approval of a majority of deputies, although constitutionally they would continue to remain responsible to the Emperor alone. The *Journal de Roubaix* (4 January 1870) was only one of the many opposition newspapers to report with glee that 'the Empire of 2 December no longer exists'. These concessions were followed by a protracted effort to create a government anxious to promote reconciliation. This was eventually formed on 2 January and headed by the former moderate republican Emile Ollivier. It would enjoy both the confidence of the Emperor and support from a parliamentary majority composed of adherents and recent liberal critics of the dynasty, including Guizot (the former Orleanist prime minister) and his erstwhile critics Barrot and Thiers. The latter, along with many liberals, might remain dissatisfied because of the retention of considerable personal, prerogative power by the Emperor (including the right to appeal by dissolution of parliament or plebiscite directly to the electorate), but conservative and liberal deputies were anxious to ensure that the achievement of their objective of exerting closer control over government policy did not excessively weaken the executive's ability to counter what was perceived to be the growing threat of revolution. The Party of Order of the Second Republic was already being re-established.

The early measures of the new Ollivier ministry were intended to satisfy its liberal critics. They included the final abandonment of the system of official candidature (23 February 1870), the dismissal of Haussmann (who had done so much to transform the centre of Paris) in order to appease conservative financial interests as well as that of the education minister, Duruy, to pacify the clerical critics of this advocate of secular instruction, together with plans for an enquiry into the impact of customs legislation. It was believed that this would represent the first step in a return to economic protectionism. Some of the most distinctive policies of the regime as well as its chosen personnel were being abandoned. The mobilisation of troops against strikers at the great Le Creusot steel and mining complex and against republican demonstrators in Paris indicated a growing and warmly welcomed determination to preserve social order. So, too, did a wave of arrests of revolutionary militants.

Indeed, for many social conservatives, including some moderate republicans, liberalisation had gone far enough. They had wanted the extension of parliamentary government and increased freedom for the press, but really only for their own sort to enjoy. According to their conception, liberty was now being abused and needed to be regulated once again. The statements made in the press of the extreme left and at public meetings in Paris, given full publicity by conservative newspapers, together with their exaggerated description of every minor disorder, contributed to the re-creation of a red scare like those of 1848 and 1851. This had the further effect of deepening an economic depression caused both by fear of internal unrest and the anxiety aroused by an unstable international situation following Prussian victory over Austria in 1866. From as early as 1867, a process of political polarisation had been underway, similar to that of 1848, and as a result of which the republicans began to assume the role of the only whole-hearted opponents of the regime. Its liberal and clerical critics increasingly subordinated their particular viewpoints to the needs of a broadly-based conservative alliance in defence of the *status quo*. According to the police *commissaire* at the southern port of Toulon (Var), 'everyone understands that the struggle which is beginning is a social conflict between those who possess and those who have nothing'. There increasingly appeared to be no alternative to support for the regime as the guarantor of social order and religion, a point reinforced by pro-government publicity during both the 1869 electoral and the 1870 plebiscite campaigns. The results of the plebiscite held on 8 May 1870 on the question concerning whether 'the people approve the liberal reforms introduced since 1860' gave some idea of the strength of this fear of social revolution.

The plebiscite campaign was relatively free of government interference, although the regime possessed considerable advantages. The Minister of the Interior, Chevandier de Valdrôme, instructed officials to employ a 'devouring activity' in support of the 'yes' vote, but not to use either pressure or threats. An unofficial *comité central plébiscitaire* presided over by the Duc d'Albufera, was established to organise the campaign. At local level, however, the habit of exerting pressure was frequently difficult to break and as always all kinds of promises of favours like new schools, roads or railway stations or threats of their denial were deployed. Private individuals and organisations also contributed. The *Est* railway company, for example, sent each of its stationmasters a copy of the Emperor's proclamation together with sufficient 'yes' ballot papers for all their staff. Typical of the official propaganda was the pro-'yes' poster distributed in the eastern department of Bas-Rhin which portrayed a peasant brandishing a tricolour flag in the one hand and rejecting a red flag with the other. The slogan, widely professed, was 'Emperor, Order and Liberty'. In general, it was the danger of revolution rather than the regime's positive achievements and liberal reforms which were stressed. Somewhat less enthusiastic, but nevertheless supporting an affirmative vote, were such newspapers as the clerical German language newspaper *Der Elsässiche Volksbote* ('The Alsatian People's Courier') published in Rixheim, which insisted that its recommendation did not represent approval of all the regime's past actions:

> We vote 'yes' because all the revolutionaries, all those who hate religion, all the oppressors of the people, all the freemasons, all the heroes of compulsory education, recommend a 'no' vote or abstention. . . . Our 'yes' is to strengthen the Emperor against the reds.

In the Gers, the *Conservateur* (26 April 1870) similarly warned that the republic which would result from a negative vote would mean 'disorder, insurrection and civil war . . . the re-establishment of the Terror . . . the 45 centime tax in permanence[1] . . . the ruin of the countryside for the profit of the towns, where the right to work acclaimed by the socialists will lead to the re-opening of the National Workshops'. Still potent memories of the revolutionary events of 1848 were thus deployed and with considerable effect.

The plebiscite was an overwhelming success for the regime. The state prosecutor at Colmar saw it as giving 'a new baptism to the Napoleonic dynasty'. There can be little doubt, in spite of the ambiguities of the plebiscatory process, that the liberal empire corresponded to the wishes of most of the population, offering as it did greater political liberty, the repression of revolutionary republicanism and, particularly to peasant voters, the promise of renewed prosperity. If most of the support for the regime came from the propertied classes and rural population, it also

---

1 A 45 per cent supplement to the land tax introduced by the republican Provisional Government in 1848.

gained substantial support from the urban middle and working classes so frequently classified among its opponents. There were a variety of reasons for this including, of course, pressure from officials or employers, but more positively because of an appreciation of improving living standards. In the case of the textile centre of Armentières in the industrial Nord, and in marked contrast with nearby Lille, there was the still attractive prospect of a 'democratic caesarism' among a working population made up largely of quite recent migrants from the countryside. The influence of the Church should not be discounted either. Whatever their misgivings about the Emperor's Italian policy, the bishops and most parish clergy felt bound to support a regime committed to social order and to protecting them from the republican menace which had spelled disaster in the past. Moreover, they had failed dismally in their efforts to attract mass support for the Papal cause. In the last analysis, although the representatives of the various conservative political groupings were divided in their response to the plebiscite, most monarchists, liberals and clericals voted 'yes' and most, but not all, moderate republicans 'no'. Nationally, there were 7, 350, 000 affirmative votes against 1, 538, 000 negative and 1, 900, 000 abstentions. The centres of opposition remained the cities. Along with Paris and the department of the Seine, Marseille and Bouches-du-Rhône was the only department to produce a majority of 'no' votes. In Paris, 59 per cent of the votes were negative – a much less decisive rejection of the regime than in the 1869 elections. The figure rose to 72–77 per cent in the predominantly working-class *arrondissements* of the north-east (11th, 18th, 19th, 20th) and to 57–71 per cent in the old revolutionary quarters of central Paris. Elsewhere, the opposition vote was substantial in the eight departments of the south-east where less than 55 per cent voted 'yes'. Support for a negative response came from all social groups, but with a heavy worker and lower-middle class preponderance. Generally, it did appear to be waning. In the relatively industrialised Nord, 75.6 per cent voted 'yes', 5.9 per cent 'no', and 16.5 per cent abstained. Even in Lille, the proportion of 'no's only reached 51 per cent (Girard 1960). Fear of social revolution had been particularly intense in the Nord and former liberal critics of the regime had been particularly active in supporting an affirmative vote. Indeed, two of their most prominent leaders, Plichon and Brame, were soon to enter the government. Everywhere republicans were bitterly disappointed. The results, nationally, indicated that a substantial majority of the population supported the regime. Whereas opposition candidates in 1869 had received 40–43 per cent of the votes cast, in the plebiscite only 17.6 per cent voted against the liberal empire. These were, of course, very different kinds of vote, but even Gambetta felt bound to admit that 'the Empire is stronger than ever'. The only viable prospect seemed to be a lengthy campaign to persuade the bourgeoisie and the rural populations that the republic did not mean revolution. The combination of concessions by the regime to its liberal and clerical critics and the appeal to their fear of revolution had successfully taken advantage of the fundamental disagreements between the various opposition groups and resulted in a major political re-alignment. The regime had escaped from the political isolation which had threatened it, and although the Bonapartist right saw the result as an opportunity for a return to an authoritarian agenda, the Emperor on 19 May, with far greater realism, re-affirmed his commitment to liberalisation.

5

Defeat and collapse

In this situation, the final collapse of the regime was to be caused by the incompetent management of foreign policy. Official and public concern about Prussian aspirations had been growing as a result of its government's hostility to French intervention in Italy in 1859, due to its support for Russian repression of the Polish revolt of 1863 and as a result of the war with Denmark in 1864. The rapidity with which Austria was defeated in 1866, however, had come as a considerable shock to the French establishment. It undoubtedly represented a major upset of the balance of power and a challenge to what had been assumed to be France's predominant position in Europe. Subsequently, relations continued to deteriorate. Napoléon III had hoped for territorial compensation for France on the left bank of the Rhine in return for his role as a mediator between Austria and Prussia, and subsequently for the cessation of Luxembourg. Failure to achieve these much publicised aspirations severely weakened the regime's internal and international reputation. Politically and militarily the balance of power was altered further, and greatly to the detriment of France, by the establishment of a Prussian dominated confederation of north German states in 1867. The subsequent negotiation of alliances between Prussia and the south German states, previously seen by French diplomats as potential allies against Prussian ambition, shifted the balance further. The outbreak of war was coming to be seen as inevitable by much of French public opinion. However, there was a clear reduction in international tension in 1869 and particularly following the establishment of the liberal Empire in 1870. Ollivier was well known for his commitment to improving relations with Prussia.

Logically a belief in the likelihood of war should have promoted an effort to ensure that the army was ready. Napoléon was fully aware of the need for military reform following the chaotic mobilisation in 1859. Prussian success in 1866 suggested an urgent need to increase the size of both the regular army and its reserves, as well as for better organisation and equipment. The question of conscription was crucial. In France, young men drew lots to determine who should join the annual contingent and serve for up to seven years. The numbers called depended on assessments of military requirements and especially budgetary constraints. It was possible, moreover, for those families who could afford the fees to purchase a replacement for unlucky participants in the ballot. On paper the system provided for an army of around 650, 000 men, but because of the regime's reluctance to increase taxation the number of conscripts called was invariably well below the army's requirements. In practice, the army in the mid-1860s was made up of 385, 000 men, of whom only around 250, 000 would have been available for front line service against a Prussian enemy. Alarmingly, in 1866 the Prussians had been able to rapidly mobilise a force of 750, 000. The problem was all too obvious. Napoléon's solution, announced in September 1866, was the Prussian one of requiring quasi-universal military service. The system of drawing lots would have been maintained with the unfortunates serving for six years followed by a period in the reserve, but with the remainder now required to serve in a reserve for six years and undergo periodic training. The objective was to create a force which, with its trained reserves, would number 1, 200, 000 (Becker and Audoin-Rouzeau 1995: 44). The proposals aroused massive opposition from the upper classes who would no longer be able to purchase exemption and the workers and peasants who had previously enjoyed the very real prospect of escaping from any kind of military obligation by drawing a *bon numéro* in the ballot. In the *Corps législatif* in December 1867, Thiers defended the principle of the professional army – well-trained and rigorously disciplined – which he claimed was more than a match for a poorly trained mass army. The left, in contrast, especially Favre and Simon, attacked the principle of permanent, repressive armies and looked back to the improvisation of 1792 for inspiration. In the face of massive parliamentary and popular opposition, faithfully reported by his own officials, Napoléon felt obliged to compromise. Those who were fortunate in the ballot would still be required to undergo some military training in a *garde nationale mobile*, but their obligations were much reduced. In practice, the disorders which resulted early in 1868 from efforts to convoke this formation for training led to the virtual abandonment of the scheme. There is an obvious paradox between the strong attachment to memories of military glory and to the achievements of the *Grande nation*, reinforced by the growing nationalist sentiment enshrined in popular education, together with the public hostility towards Prussia and the widespread belief that war was inevitable and the unwillingness to meet either the financial or personal obligations necessary to strengthen the army.

The decision to engage in a hazardous war was nevertheless the Emperor's responsibility, although the role of public opinion should not be ignored. The crisis when it arose would be unexpected, short and intense. The conservative press responded in bellicose terms to the announcement on 3 July of the candidature of the Prussian Prince Leopold for the Spanish throne. Hohenzollern monarchs on the Rhine and Pyrenean frontiers appeared to threaten encirclement. Although the Emperor and Ollivier might have been willing to accept a simple Prussian withdrawal of this candidature, conservatives in the *Corps législatif* demanded guarantees which the Prussian chancellor Bismarck refused in terms calculated to enflame the situation in the famous Ems telegram. Another humiliating foreign policy reversal and a possible parliamentary defeat would have thrown the bases of the revised constitution, and particularly the Emperor's personal power, into doubt. In these circumstances Napoléon and Ollivier appear to have weakly accepted the advice of the Empress, the foreign minister the Duc de Gramont, and the more authoritarian Bonapartists to opt for war in the hope that victory would further consolidate the regime. Military credits – in effect a declaration of war – were voted by the *Corps législatif* on 15 July: 245 deputies voted in favour, ten against and seven abstained revealing that many republicans and almost the entire liberal opposition had rallied. The initial public response was quite positive, throughout the country, and especially in the towns, although this was probably as much out of a sense of resignation rather than real enthusiasm. In Paris and frontier departments in the north-east, where people still remembered the cruelty of the Prussian occupiers in 1815, huge crowds gathered in the streets to see the troops leave for the front, singing patriotic songs, including – by special permission of the Interior Ministry – the republican hymn, the *Marseillaise*. With the exception of a small minority of revolutionary militants, even republicans felt obliged to rally to the cause of national defence. There was every confidence in the ability of the army to achieve rapid victory. Recently, historians have pointed to the development of an embryonic 'Sacred Union' in 1870 similar to that of

1914. Peasants appear to have become Frenchmen well before the Third Republic despite arguments to the contrary by the American historian, Eugen Weber. Only the extreme left, not represented in parliament and more then ever isolated in this situation, continued to manifest an irreconcilable opposition to both the regime and what they perceived to be *its* war. Even so, this apparent union concealed efforts by the various political groupings to improve their situation. Above all, in 1870 there were the efforts of the authoritarian Bonapartists, marginalised in the precious year's elections, to reverse the liberalising trend and weaken the Ollivier government.

Reports of a French victory, in an insignificant engagement at Sarrebrück on 2 August, were greeted with great enthusiasm. The first defeats on 4 and 6 August were a massive shock. Rumours spread and with them panic. In Paris, Lyon and Marseille during the first two weeks of August demonstrators had already begun to call for the Republic as the only means of saving France. The Emperor's response to the deepening military crisis was to replace the Ollivier ministry on 9 August with a government made up of authoritarian Bonapartists under General Cousin-Montauban. At the same time, efforts were made to mobilise more men and to re-establish popular morale. It was too late. The French army had gone to war suffering from major structural weaknesses, compounded by the absence of reform. One of the paradoxes of the situation was that the Emperor had been well aware of these deficiencies and still had chosen to risk war. The army was, in practice, better prepared to deal with internal security problems than with a major European campaign. In terms of its training and equipment, it was unprepared. Its mobilisation procedures resulted in chaos. It suffered from a catastrophic lack of central coordination and the Emperor's presence with the armies and constant interference only made this worse. Certainly, he had not inherited his uncle's military genius. *Elan*, frontal attacks and the spirit of improvisation, of muddling through, would cost the army dearly. The heroic efforts of its officers and men were no compensation for the high command's inability to achieve the strategic concentration of its forces which alone might have compensated for numerical inferiority.

In an effort to relieve the army of the Rhine which was encircled at Metz, Napoléon and Marshal MacMahon led another army into a trap at Sedan. The Emperor surrendered on 2 September. News of this humiliating capitulation was received in Paris on the evening of 3 September and became public knowledge during the following day. The contrast with past military glory was extreme. With this the Empire lost all credit.

It simply faded away. Catastrophic defeat had destroyed its claims to legitimacy. In this political vacuum, the small group of 27 republican deputies in the *Corps législatif* demanded the replacement of the regime. They were supported by crowds which on 4 September, as in 1848, invaded the Palais Bourbon. There was no resistance and no bloodshed. Troops and police guarding the building had been unwilling to resort to force against the demonstrators in such an uncertain political situation. The more moderate among the republican *députés de Paris* seized their opportunity and established a Provisional Government of National Defense partly to prevent the much feared seizure of power by the Parisian revolutionaries, partly from a determination to re-organise the military effort. This would be presided over by the military governor of Paris, General Trochu. A similar, unopposed republican take-over had occurred in Lyon and Marseille even before the news of events in the capital had been received. Elsewhere, in the provinces news of military defeat and revolution frequently came as a great surprise. The Imperial administration collapsed and only the republicans had the organisation and record of consistent opposition which allowed them to present themselves as the legitimate successors to the Empire. Thus, Republican notables were able to take over local administration virtually without opposition. There were odd exceptions: at Tourcoing (Nord) workers demonstrated against their employers, and peasants in a number of places were reported to have complained that the Emperor had been 'betrayed by the rich and the republicans' (Corbin 1992). Generally, even the conservative press, like the *Mémorial de Lille* (5 September) called for unity in defence of the nation. If the liberal Empire had attracted substantial support from all social groups, and in particular had satisfied the demand of the social elites for a greater role in decision making, military defeat represented governmental failure on a scale sufficient to destroy the regime's legitimacy.

6

Conclusion

After Sedan, Napoléon remained a prisoner in Germany for over six months, until his release in March 1871. Subsequently, he established his family in England, in a mansion at Camden Place, Chiselhurst. There he began to plan another *coup d'état*, but the continued deterioration of his health made this an unrealistic prospect. He died on 9 January 1873 following an operation to remove a stone from his bladder. This was not, however, the end of Bonapartism. The outbreak of the Paris Commune, within days of the deposed ruler's arrival in Britain, which culminated in the slaughter of 20, 000 men and women by the former imperial army, released from its German prisoner-of-war camps for the purpose, revealed once more the intensity of social fear within the elites and the potential for conflict in French society. The death of the discredited Emperor had left Bonapartists with an attractive candidate for the throne in the person of his son, born in 1856. By 1874, a propaganda campaign in favour of the Prince-Imperial supported by over 70 newspapers and an outpouring of pamphlets and prints was being organised by former pillars of the Empire such as Rouher and Pietri. In the general election of January–March 1876, some 75 Bonapartist deputies were elected, notably in the south-west. At its peak in October 1877, there were 104 Bonapartist deputies. They were overwhelmingly conservative and clerical, wealthy and paternalistic, and enjoying solid local political bases – men like Granier de Cassagnac in Gers, Echassériaux in Charente and the Baron de Bourgoigne in the Nièvre. Elsewhere, although much of the previous popular support for a democratic Bonapartism was draining away to the republicans, a latent sympathy survived. This continued to associate the Empire with prosperity and attracted support in regions as diverse as the cereal cultivating plains of the Beauce in the Paris basin and the vineyards of the Hérault. There were also many sympathisers within the bureaucracy and the army. However, with the futile death of the Prince-Imperial in Africa, fighting the Zulus with the British army, the movement largely expired.

How should we conclude? Previous assessments have very much reflected historians' personalities and contemporaneous public concerns. These have ranged from the political stability of the early Third Republic to the need to promote economic development and political stability during the inter-war depression and the period of post-war reconstruction, as well as the emergence of de Gaulle at the head of another 'Bonapartist' regime. The label has been used as an explanatory category by both historians and political sociologists, and as a term of abuse by politicians and journalists. In the aftermath of the mid-century crisis, given the intensity of the social fear caused by the 1848 Revolution, the preference of elites for a strong authoritarian government was not surprising. Conservatives would probably have made a pact with the devil in order to safeguard their property and privileges. Indeed, much wider sections of the population desperately desired a return to order and prosperity, to 'normality' as they conceived it. The parallels with Germany in 1933 and the rise of Hitler are, in this respect, striking. The authoritarian option carried substantial risks, however. It involved granting considerable power to a single individual, an opportunist with his own agenda, his own strengths and weaknesses. Moreover, effective government would depend on the ruler's physical and mental well-being and Napoléon III's capacity to rule was soon reduced by persistent ill-health and premature ageing. In the longer term, the dangers of personal rule would become increasingly apparent to many erstwhile supporters of the regime, in a series of policy decisions which appeared contrary to the interests of powerful vested interest groups. From personal inclination, and under pressure, Napoléon III was at least prepared to adapt and to engage in a process of transition from authoritarianism towards a more liberal political system. Recent experience in Eastern Europe has provided some insights into the difficulties involved. A sense of expectancy builds up which is difficult to satisfy. Latent tensions once again are openly displayed as pressure from above eases and as social and political groups feel able to compete for power. What had begun as a series of voluntary concessions made possible by the regime's success against the menace of revolution, very rapidly turned into enforced concessions to pressure from the socio-political elites upon whose collaboration the regime depended. Moreover, the impact of these reforms was always reduced by the Emperor's continued determination to pursue his personal policies at the expense of what important business circles as well as the Church and its clerical supporters saw as their vital interests. Taken together with a succession of foreign policy failures, this ensured widening support for the reinforcement of parliamentary control over the errant monarch. Unable to win over the urban masses and faced with a gradual weakening in the loyalty of the rural population, the Emperor finally conceded a 'liberal' constitution which, while retaining much of his personal power especially in matters of defence and foreign policy, substantially reinforced the potential for parliamentary control. In spite of this substantial weakening of Napoléon's personal power, and the accompanying decline in his prestige, the plebiscite in May 1870 had seemed to mark a new beginning. Even then, if war had been avoided a liberal empire still would have encountered considerable difficulty. However, this is mere speculation. The propensity for war was an integral part of Bonapartism as defined by Napoléon III. But success in waging war depended on military efficiency and neither the organisation of the French army nor the quality of its leadership made it fit for war against Prussia. If, then, the experience of the Second Empire offers a lesson, it is simply that authoritarian government (while it might appear to offer an attractive solution in a moment of intense social crisis) is, due to the brutality of its origins, more likely to reinforce than reduce social and political divisions and, in the longer term, is likely to prove to be an extremely inefficient and dangerous method of conducting affairs.

Bibliography

Setting the context

Caron, F. *La France des patriotes de 1851 à 1914* (1985).
Becker, J.-J. and Audoin-Rouzeau, S. *La France, la Nation, la Guerre: 1850–1920* (1995).
Charle, C. *A Social History of France in the Nineteenth Century* (1994).
Gibson, R. *A Social History of French Catholicism, 1789–1914* (1989).
McPhee, P. *A Social History of France, 1780–1880* (1992).
Magraw, R. *France , 1815–1914. The Bourgeois Century* (1983).
Price, R. *A Social History of Nineteenth Century France* (1987).
—— 'France: the search for stability' in B. Waller (ed.) *Themes in Modern European History, 1830–90* (1990).
Tombs, R. *France, 1814–1914* (1996).
Weber, E. *Peasants into Frenchmen* (1976).

The presidency of Louis-Napoléon Bonaparte

Agulhon, M. *The Republican Experiment, 1848–52* (1983).
Apponyi, R. *De la révolution au coup d'état*, Geneva (1948).
Dansette, A. *Louis Napoléon à la conquête du pouvoir* (1961).
Lévêque, P. *Société en crise. La Bourgogne de la Monarchie de Juillet au Second Empire*, 2 vols, (1983).
Marx, K. 'The Eighteenth Brumaire of Louis Bonaparte' in *Marx–Engels Selected Works*, I, Moscow (1962).
Margadant, T. *French Peasants in Revolt: the Insurrection of 1851* (1979).
Merriman, J.M. *The Agony of the Republic: the Repression of the Left in Revolutionary France 1848–51* (1978).
Normanby, Lord *Journal of the Year of Revolution*, 2 vols, (1851)

67

Price, R. *The French Second Republic. A Social History* (1972).

—— (ed.) *Revolution and Reaction: 1848 and the Second French Republic* (1975).

de Rémusat, C. *Mémoires de ma vie*, IV, (1962).

Senior, N.W. *Journals Kept in France and Italy from 1848 to 1852*, 2 vols, (1871).

de Tocqueville, A. *Recollections*, J.P. Mayer (ed.) (1959).

Tudesq, A.J. *L'Election présidentielle de Louis-Napoléon Bonaparte 10 décembre 1848* (1965).

General studies of the Second Empire

Campbell, S. *The Second Empire Revisited: A Study in French Historiography* (1978).

Echard, W. (ed.) *Historical Dictionary of the French Second Empire* (1985).

Girard, L. *Napoléon III* (1986).

McMillan, J. *Napoleon III* (1991).

Plessis, A. *The Rise and Fall of the Second Empire 1852–71* (1985).

Senior, N.W. *Conversations with M. Thiers, M. Guizot and other Distinguished Persons during the Second Empire*, 2 vols, (1878).

Smith, W.H.C. *Second Empire and Commune: France 1848–71* (1985).

—— *Napoleon III. The Pursuit of Prestige* (1991).

Tulard, J. *Dictionnaire du Second Empire* (1995).

Zeldin, T. *The Political System of Napoleon III* (1958).

More specialised studies

Anderson, R. *Education in France 1848–70* (1971).

Aminzade, R. *Ballots and Barricades. Class Formation and Republican Politics in France, 1830–71* (1993).

Audoin-Rouzeau, S. *1870, La France dans la guerre* (1989).

Bernard, M. 'La réoganisation de la police sous le Second Empire' in P. Vigier *et al.* (eds), *Maintien de l'ordre et police en France et en Europe au 19e siècle* (1987).

Bury, J. and Tombs, R. *Thiers, 1797–1877. A political life* (1986).

Case, L. *French Opinion on War and Diplomacy during the Second Empire* (1954).

Corbin, A. *The Village of Cannibals: Rage and murder in France, 1870* (1992).

Delotel, A. *et al. Aux origines de la Commune: le mouvement des réunions publiques à Paris, 1868–70* (1980).

Duveau, G. *La Vie ouvrière en France sous le Second Empire* (1946).

Echard, W. *Napoleon III and the Concert of Europe* (1983).

Emerit, M. (ed.) *Lettres de Napoléon III à Madame Cornu* (1937).

Girard, L. *La Politique des travaux publics du Second Empire* (1951).

—— (ed.) *Les Elections de 1869* (1960).

Girard, L., Prost, A. and Gossez, R. *Les Conseillers généraux en 1870: étude statistique d'un personnel politique* (1967).

Gough, A. *Paris and Rome: the Gallican Church and the Ultramontane Campaign 1848–53* (1986).

Gould, R. *Insurgent Identities. Class, Community, and Protest in Paris from 1848 to the Commune* (1995).

Holmes, R. *The Road to Sedan: the French Army 1866–70* (1984).

Kulstein, D. *Napoleon III and the Working Class: A Study of Government Propaganda under the Second Empire* (1969).

Le Clère, B. and Wright,V. *Les Préfets du Second Empire* (1973).

L'Huillier, F. *La Lutte ouvrière à la fin du Second Empire* (1957).

Magraw, R. *A History of the French Working Class*,Vol. I, (1992).

Maurain, J. *La Politique ecclésiastique du Second Empire de 1852 à 1869* (1930).

Ménager, B. *Les Napoléons du peuple* (1988).

Palmade, G. 'Le départment du Gers à la fin du Second Empire' in *Bulletin de la Société archéologique, historique et scientifique du Gers* (1961).

Payne, H.C. *The Police State of Louis Napoleon Bonaparte 1851–60* (1965).

Pinkney, D. *Napoleon III and the Re-building of Paris* (1958).

Pottinger, E. *Napoleon III and the German Crisis 1865–66* (1966).

Price, R. *The Modernization of Rural France. Communication networks and agricultural market structures in nineteenth century France* (1983).

Ratcliffe, B. 'Napoleon III and the Anglo-French Commercial Treaty of 1860: a reconsideration' in B. Ratcliffe (ed.) *Great Britain and her World 1750–1914* (1975).

Rougerie, J. *et al. La 1re Internationale* (1964).

Steefel, L. *Bismarck, the Hohenzollern Candidacy, and the Origins of the Franco-German War* (1962).

Tchernoff, I. *Le Parti républicain au coup d'état et sous le Second Empire* (1906).

Wright, V. 'La loi de sûreté générale de 1858' in *Revue d'histoire moderne et contemporaine* (1969).

—— *Le Conseil d'Etat sous le Second Empire* (1972).

—— 'Les Préfets de police pendant le Second Empire' in *L'Etat et sa police en France* (1979).

Zeldin, T. *Emile Ollivier and the Liberal Empire* (1963).

—— (ed.) *Conflicts in French Society: Anti-clericalism, education and morals in the 19th century* (1970).

Local and regional studies

Armengaud, A. *Les Populations de l'est-Aquitain au début de l'époque contemporaine* (1961).

Boivin, M. *Le Mouvement ouvrier dans la région de Rouen 1851–76*, 2 vols, (1989).

Corbin, A. *Archaisme et modernité en Limousin au 19e siècle*, 2 vols, (1975).

Dupeux, G. *Aspects de l'histoire sociale et politique du Loir-et-Cher* (1962).

Gaillard, J. *Paris, la ville (1852–70)* (1977).

Girard, L. *Nouvelle histoire de Paris. La deuxième république et le second empire* (1981).

Gordon, D. *Merchants and Capitalists. Industrialization and Provincial Politics in mid-nineteenth France* (1985).

Harvey, D. *Consciousness and the Urban Experience* (1985).

Huard, R. *Le Mouvement républicain en Bas-Languedoc, 1848–81* (1982).

Igersheim, F. *Politique et administration dans le Bas-Rhin 1848–70* (1993).

Launay, M. *Le Diocèse de Nantes sous le Second Empire*, 2 vols, (1982).

Marcilhacy, C. *Le Diocèse d'Orléans sous l'épiscopat de Mgr. Dupanloup* (1962).

Ménager, B. *La Vie politique dans le département du Nord de 1851 à 1877* (1977).

Pierrard, P. *La Vie ouvrière à Lille sous le Second Empire* (1965).

Vigreux, M. *Paysans et notables du Morvan au 19e siècle* (1987).